Splashing
in Life's Puddles

Cathryn M. Scott

WestBow
PRESS

A DIVISION OF THOMAS NELSON

WestBow Press books may be ordered through booksellers or by contacting:

WestBow Press
A Division of Thomas Nelson
1663 Liberty Drive
Bloomington, IN 47403
www.westbowpress.com
1-(866) 928-1240

Because of the dynamic nature of the Internet, any web addresses or links contained in
this book may have changed since publication and may no longer be valid. The views
expressed in this work are solely those of the author and do not necessarily reflect the
views of the publisher, and the publisher hereby disclaims any responsibility for them.

Any people depicted in stock imagery provided by Thinkstock are models,
and such images are being used for illustrative purposes only.

Certain stock imagery © Thinkstock.

ISBN: 978-1-4497-6077-9 (sc)

Library of Congress Control Number: 2012914288

Printed in the United States of America

WestBow Press rev. date: 08/14/2012

"Life isn't about waiting for the storm to pass... it's about learning to dance in the rain." After that just splash in life's puddles!

Contents

Introduction

After the dust had settled following my second divorce and the boxes had been unpacked in my new apartment, I stood at my living room window and looked out at the beautiful mountains that overlooked the river down below. I sighed as I gazed out the window and then asked myself, "Why do you always pick the wrong person to marry?" I was in my mid-40s and did not want to try for a third time. But I did want to understand why I had been unable to select a suitable mate. At first glance, my two husbands were complete opposites so I obviously didn't go after the same type every time.

My second husband was a hard worker, and my first husband hardly worked. My second husband was a doctor, and my first husband dropped out of high school and later got a GED. My second husband didn't have wandering eyes, whereas my first husband was always on the lookout for something better. My second husband came home every night for dinner – my first husband staggered home hours after the dinner dishes were washed and put away. My second husband idolized his young daughter and never wanted to leave her side. My first husband left his 5-year-old daughter behind when he found a woman he wanted to be with more.

So what about their similarities? Both were good looking and intelligent men. Husband #1 was a charming, tall, and handsome man with blue eyes who had multiple talents. There probably wasn't a musical instrument he couldn't play and he could sing as well. He was artistic. He was also a fantastic cook. There wasn't any job he couldn't do once he set his mind to it. The problem was, his biggest dream was to make it big in the music world. He thought he could someday take Nashville by storm. So when that didn't work out, he was on the lookout for the perfect get-rich-quick scheme. He never made much money because he didn't stick with anything long enough to earn a good salary. Earning an honest living by working steadily never appealed to him. This is in addition to his never-ending quest to find the perfect woman. The last I heard he was still looking. His conquests are now around the age of our oldest grandson.

Husband #2 was also a handsome man of average height with dark brown eyes and jet black hair. He was very friendly but sometimes a bit awkward socially and therefore lacked the smooth-talking charisma needed to charm other women. He was a gifted dentist who was serious about his profession and cared about his patients. He wasn't musically talented like Husband #1, but he had a nice singing voice and would often burst into song to entertain our children. One of my favorite memories is of him enthusiastically belting out the words to a song called "Lean on Me!" Until mental illness took its toll, he went to work faithfully every day. He is currently living in a small apartment and receives Social Security Disability. His monthly checks are handled by family members who supervise his spending.

So what did these two men have in common? Neither one felt my needs deserved any recognition. They were never able or willing to offer emotional support or treat me as an important person in their life. I didn't feel or enjoy the security of being loved. The vow to love, honor, and cherish turned out to be an empty promise. Neither one of my marriages was a true partnership. They treated me the way my father had treated me and I hung in there the way my mother had done with my father. This was my legacy.

I saw a poster that said something about getting through life's storms by learning to dance in the rain. Right. Like I was going to dance a jig as I hurried off to bankruptcy court. Or I was going to break into an old tap dancing routine while waiting by the side of the road for the tow truck. Oh, and how about twirling gracefully around the living room while my husband was out with another woman. I don't think so. But then I thought about it and realized what it really meant. It meant to not let life's storms beat you to a pulp and leave you lying in a helpless heap on the floor.

OK. I guess I learned to dance in the rain because I survived all that life threw at me and I was stronger than ever as a result. In fact, I was more than that. I was feeling very happy and carefree. I must be splashing in life's puddles.

Chapter 1

It All Began Innocently Enough.....

I was raised in a college town in upstate New York during the 40s and 50s. Anyone who can recall growing up during this time period knows what an uncomplicated life we had back then.

I remember a neighborhood filled with other children and playing outside until we were all called in for dinner. Some nights we were allowed to play outside after it got dark and we caught fireflies. I learned to ride a bike by having my mother run huffing and puffing alongside as I struggled to pedal up and down the street. I guess they didn't have training wheels back then. In the summer she would often pack our wooden picnic basket with potato salad and hot dogs and buns so we could eat dinner at a local park when my dad came home from work. Toys and games were simple. I enjoyed playing paper dolls with my mother or "house" with my dolls. I took piano lessons and had daily practice sessions under my mother's watchful eye. I took tap dancing lessons and practiced by cranking up the record player called a Victrola and then placing the over-sized needle carefully on the big, black record as it spun out songs like "Daughter of Rosie O'Grady" or "Under the Double Eagle." In the evening we would gather in the living room and listen to programs like Jack Benny or Arthur Godfrey on our great big radio that was the size of a small cabinet.

When I was in third grade I had my first encounter with politics. Dwight (Ike) Eisenhower was running for president. I recall that many times my friends and I would scream "WE LIKE IKE" at the top of our lungs on the school bus. (Poor bus driver!) Another time I remember being in school and having the school's dental hygienist clean my teeth. I asked her if she were a Republican or a Democrat, not having any idea what the difference was except that my parents were Republicans. When she said to me in a firm voice, "I'm a *Democrat!*" I was suddenly alarmed because I thought anyone who wasn't a Republican was a Communist and they were the bad guys.

Mothers were central in a child's life because they all stayed home and took care of the children and did housework. I grew up thinking fathers were to be feared because mine definitely was. He was tall and big and not friendly. I grew up especially afraid of men in work clothes, your basic blue collar worker.

One time I remember seeing two of my playmates joyfully greet their father when he came home from work. They ran into his arms and he gave them a great big hug with a smile. I tried doing that once to my father, but it didn't work as well; he shoved me aside. So much for that.

He was strange in another way. He never used my mother's first name. He'd said "Hey" if he wanted her for something, but he never once called her by her first name or even, Honey. Also, we weren't allowed to call her Mommy. I heard my friends calling their moms "Mommy" but when I tried it, my father quickly admonished me by saying "Her name is Mother." My father was completely uninterested in his children and left everything to my mother. My mother was undoubtedly very unhappy even in those early years, but divorce was practically unheard of back then. One time I remember hearing that a neighbor lady of ours was divorced, and I immediately wondered what SHE had done wrong that her husband didn't stay with her.

My father went to work every day, carrying his black lunch box that my mother had packed for him. As a little girl, I grew up with the idea of marrying a man who would go to work every day while I stayed home and took care of our children, just like my mother. That's the way we thought back in those days.

I was not unhappy as a child. Being ignored by my father while my mother took care of my brother and me was very normal. My mother was lively and energetic, and my father was the complete opposite. She loved people and having friends over and going places while he preferred to stay home and be left alone.

My father was the oldest of five children born to Hungarian immigrants. He developed a huge resentment with his parents when his youngest sibling was born because my father was told to move down the street and sleep at his grandparents' house since there wasn't enough room for everyone. My mother said he spent most of his time at his parents' house and took his meals there but had a bedroom at his grandparents' house a few doors down. Whenever my mother would ask him about his childhood, he became very angry and wouldn't talk so no one knows the real story. But apparently he never forgave them and avoided family gatherings at my grandparents' house all together.

My mother's parents divorced about a year after my mother was born. Her father took off and disappeared. Her mother was a very beautiful and artistically gifted young woman, but was totally incapable of raising a child alone so my mother went to live with her maternal grandparents, who later became her legal guardians. When she became a teenager she went to live with her wealthy aunt and uncle, who were strict and unloving. They turned her back over to her grandparents when she graduated from high school.

Because her own childhood had been so fractured, she wanted my younger brother and me to be connected with our extended family. Even though my father refused to accompany us, my mother frequently took us to see our paternal grandparents so we could spend time with our cousins and aunts and uncles who were usually there as well. They lived in a well manicured neighborhood along with immigrants from several other countries. I enjoyed playing with my cousins and seeing my aunts and uncles. One of them was an uncle who was my father's look-alike brother. They could have passed for twins. It always seemed strange to me to see someone who looked just like my father laugh and play with his three daughters.

My mother felt it was important for us to know her side of the family as well so she occasionally took my brother and me to visit her mother. Visiting this grandmother was always interesting. She eventually remarried and had six more children. The family was financially destitute and lived in squalor with no indoor plumbing. I remember visiting my grandmother when my aunts and uncles (my mother's half siblings) were a happy but rowdy bunch of teenagers and young adults. They were a noisy bunch who seemed to be constantly going in and out of the house. I developed a big crush on one of my uncles because he was very charming and good looking, but more than that, he paid attention to me. One time he tried to teach me how to yodel but I never mastered it. Still though, in order to be like him and to have him like me, I worked on it when I was at home. I wanted to marry him when I grew up. He was my prince charming.

I'm sure my mother was beyond uncomfortable whenever we visited their home because she had been raised in a strict environment and taught to observe proper etiquette and to conduct herself in a socially acceptable manner. She had also been raised to practice rigid personal hygiene. Her mother's family was the total opposite. Her need to maintain contact with her mother and siblings, however, overshadowed what we experienced when we went to visit. She wanted my brother and me to know our grandmother and our aunts and uncles and for them to know us.

My mother tried her best to make my father happy and to take care of him but they were such opposites that it never worked. Her bubbly personality was in direct contrast to that of my father. When my mother would be chatting happily with others, my father would remain quiet and in the background. However, if she made a statement such as "Jack was just delighted that ......" or "Jack was so thrilled......" or "Jack was really excited......" he would angrily jump in with, "I WAS NOT DELIGHTED....." or whatever word she had used that indicated any sort of enthusiasm on his part. Heaven forbid he should be seen as happy or positive about anything!! As I got older it became quite amusing to watch his reaction to her outgoing personality. As for compliments? They were non-existent. If my mother asked my father if he liked a particular meal we were eating, he'd respond, "It's fit to eat." That's as close as he ever came to giving her a compliment.

I do remember one time when my parents displayed a bit of affection. We were going somewhere in the car. From my observation point in the back seat, I noticed my mother was sitting close to my father and he had his arm around her. Back in those days there were no seat belts or bucket seats. I was quite impressed that he was able to steer with only one hand and when I asked him about it, he playfully responded: "I can steer with my knees!" We all laughed. It is a tiny snapshot memory of a happy moment that I've never forgotten.

My brother was born with club feet that required a lot of medical attention. He had several operations and I can remember his legs being encased in casts. When he wasn't in casts, he wore sturdy shoes with a big metal bar between them. When that therapy ended, he had to wear his shoes on the wrong feet to continue to straighten them out.

His many surgeries and casts and later expensive special shoes were a financial burden on any household budget back in those days. One day my father asked his father for financial help to buy the expensive special shoes my brother required and he was told *no, a man should take care of his own family.* This had to have hurt him when his father turned him down but instead of deciding he would never do that to *his* family and hurt his children in the same manner, he carried that same attitude to his children so that whenever I asked for help, my request was flatly denied. However, my mother did override this on a few occasions when my first marriage ended.

In the 50s I became a teenager and developed a close circle of friends with some of the girls and boys from our church, the Willow Glen Community Church. There were five of us girls, and I was the youngest. One summer we snuck out of our homes several nights to meet the boys who were camping out. Back in those days it was all just a lot of innocent giggling and kissing. No alcohol. No smoking. No sex. Just the thrill of doing something naughty like sneaking out of the house while our parents slept was excitement enough. Our innocent adventures came to an end the night my mother intervened. One of the girls was supposed to call me when she got home from babysitting but I fell asleep and my mother answered the phone. When my mother softly answered, my friend whispered that she was ready. My mom then whispered, "OK" and hung up. She walked down the hall to my bedroom and woke me up and told me I'd better call my friend back and tell her it had been my mother who answered the phone, not me. Oh boy!!! My friend was SO embarrassed to face my mother in church the next day. But it sure was great fun while it lasted.

My best friend and I were forever having parties in our homes. Hers were held in her living room, and mine were held in our basement. Parents, of course, were *always* home in other parts of the house. We'd have lots of soda and chips and all the latest records. We'd put on a touch of pink lipstick and lower the lights. It was a fun time and all so very different from today's teenage parties.

I had a boyfriend among my Willow Glen friends and fell in love for the first time. This turned out to be the beginning of many relationships where I was treated poorly and gratefully accepted any crumbs that were thrown in my direction. He was a little older and loved to take advantage of my vulnerability. Take, for example, the school bus ride in the morning. My stop was before his and he knew I was waiting and hoping for him to sit down beside me when the bus got to his house. I would hold my breath as the door opened and he climbed up the steps knowing it would go one of two ways. He would either walk down the aisle and glance in my direction and sit down beside me or ignore me completely and walk by as if I didn't exist. When he didn't sit with me, I was totally crushed and stared sullenly out the window the rest of the ride to school. He graduated from high school before me and I did eventually overcome my first love.

After that I dated several boys during my high school years but only one totally captured my heart. His name was Jeff Wood. We met in junior high and I noticed him because he always wore dark pants, a white long-sleeved dress shirt, and had a guitar in his locker. Plus, he was tall, very good looking and had the most beautiful blue eyes I'd ever seen. He swept me off my feet by making me feel as if no one else in the world mattered except me. Unfortunately, his family moved to Pennsylvania just as I was entering high school, and I was devastated. But Jeff turned out to be a prolific letter writer with beautiful handwriting to match, and we wrote literally hundreds of letters to each other over the next several years. For awhile his letters arrived daily. Then life would take over and we would get involved with our high school activities and friends, and Jeff would fade to the background. He had an older brother who was out of high school and working at a full time job. He decided to remain in New York after the family moved to Pennsylvania so Jeff returned every summer to visit his brother and to see me. This pattern continued all the way through high school.

If I were dating someone when Jeff came back to town, I dropped everything to be with him. When summer was over and he returned home to begin the next school year, we wrote letters daily that eventually tapered off as the year wore on. He was a year ahead of me in school and joined the Navy when he got out of high school.

In June of 1961, I graduated from high school and went to school for a year in New York City at a prestigious business school. The summer after my high school graduation my mother and I shopped for business suits, shoes, hats, gloves, and a briefcase according to the instructions that came with my acceptance letter. Finally the day arrived for my mother and me to board a bus for NYC with my suitcases full of new clothes, high heeled shoes, and accessories. My "dorm" was a luxurious hotel for women. When we arrived, I approached the front desk and was told my room number. Off we went in search of the elevators and my new room. My mother helped me put everything away in my closet, medicine cabinet, and dresser drawers and before I knew it, she was back on a bus returning home. I was on my own for the first time in my life.

I began to meet the other girls as they arrived and moved into their rooms up and down the hall. We immediately began to bond and make plans to explore the city together. We had private rooms with our own phone and maid service. In the morning I would dress in my business suit and heels and take the elevator to the dining room where Mitzi, my favorite waitress, would hurry to bring my breakfast to me as soon as she saw me come into the room. Although we could sit wherever we wanted, most of us ate at the same table with the same group of girls every morning. After breakfast I took the elevator back to my room where I would brush my teeth, put on lipstick and my hat, grab my briefcase and white gloves and either take a taxi with several classmates or take a bus if I wasn't running late to our school rooms which were located in the Grand Central Station building. The Pan Am building was under construction at this time, and when the workmen saw us hurrying down the sidewalk holding brief cases and slapping hats on our heads at the last minute they would stop what they were doing and yell to each other, "Here they come!" Then they would gawk and stare at us as we hurried into the building. Our presence stood out because we were the only young girls who wore business suits, hats, and gloves. During the first few weeks, we would come home at night in so much pain from wearing high heeled shoes all day that we would remove them after getting off the bus and limp down the sidewalk back to the hotel in our stockings. We then hobbled to our rooms to soak our aching feet. By the end of the year we were pros and could wear high heeled shoes 24/7.

The work was very demanding, but business subjects came easily and naturally to me, so I loved it. The challenge was to become the fastest typist on the manual typewriters and the fastest student in shorthand. I actually did achieve the latter goal. But in addition to the business courses, there were lessons in walking, answering the phone, being a good hostess for your boss at important meetings, and learning to think ahead of the boss to anticipate his every need. The boss was always a man and our job was to make his easier.

Lunch consisted of stopping with my best friend for a hot dog at the street vendor and then going to the automat for pie and coffee. When our lunch hour was over we'd hurry back for our afternoon classes.

After dinner, evenings were spent doing hours of homework. The most dreaded homework was the typing assignment. We had to type the assignment on 11" x 14" paper *without an error.* We could not erase. We had to start over, even if we made a mistake on the very last line. Talk about nights of tears and exasperation!!! But we also had time to enjoy each other's company in our rooms where we would share whatever snacks we had stashed away in our dresser drawers and just act like silly 19 year olds. My best friend and I shared a birthday so we were "twins" and celebrated our 19th birthday together. Students were allowed to go out any night they wanted, but we had a curfew and had to sign out and then back in using the book that was on a small table by the elevators.

Sometimes a bunch of us girls would go as a group to Malachy's, a friendly, neighborhood bar within walking distance of the hotel. We also attended performances at Radio City Music Hall, visited Chinatown, and strolled through Central Park. On Saturday afternoons, if I were feeling homesick for the greenery and scenery of home, I would go to Central Park and feed the squirrels and read my mail.

Although I had fun with the girls, I had an inner yearning for a boyfriend. I didn't feel complete without a male in my life. For the first time I was in an all-girls school with no boys in sight and I didn't think I could make it without a boyfriend. This yearning had nothing at all to do with sex. It was about having a boy validate my existence and tell me I was loved and mattered to him. It was feeling as if there were someone in my immediate world who cared about me and thought I was important.

There were mixers with other NYC students, and that's where I met a young, blonde-haired man named Carl. He wasn't a student so I'm not sure why he was at this particular event. He was a reporter for *Life Magazine*. I dated him for several weeks and would frequently take the subway to Greenwich Village to hang out with him in his apartment. But by the end of the year, he ended up with a fellow student. Here's how that happened. One night he called the hotel to talk to me and the operator connected him to the wrong room. He ended up talking to this other girl for quite awhile and they hit it off. They agreed to meet and eventually they ended up together. I was really hurt and felt betrayed when they told me several weeks later.

In the hotel, a large living room on one of the top floors with several couches and chairs and a TV was reserved exclusively for my school. The day John Glenn circled the earth in a rocket-ship I was "home" sick with a cold. I had called the school to report I would not be attending and then, still clad in my pajamas, bathrobe and slippers, and armed with a box of tissues, I took the elevator up to our living room and watched the breathtaking events unfold on TV. Another memory is having tea on the Mezzanine. This was an opportunity to learn to hone our social skills. There was a strict dress code that did not allow casual attire. We nibbled little cookies while we sipped our tea out of china cups and made small talk. Men were not allowed beyond the lobby so they would call our rooms using one of the phones in the lobby to indicate they were there to pick us up for a date or whatever. We then went downstairs in the elevator to meet them. It was all so very proper.

We had a big formal dance in the spring at the Waldorf Astoria. By this time, I was dating a graduate student from one of the universities back home where my mother was working as a secretary. He was from another country and was truly tall, dark, and handsome. I can no longer remember how we met or when we started dating but I'm thinking it might have been on one of my visits home for a holiday and perhaps my mother introduced us. But we knew each other well enough for him to agree to come to NYC to escort me to the dance and brought a friend for my best friend. We had such a great time.

Finals were grueling, and we had to pass a series of tests in classes such as shorthand, typing, and bookkeeping with a certain grade before we could certify and return home. There was no formal graduation ceremony. The certification process began in mid-May, and everyone had until sometime in June to complete the tests. My best friend and I and just a few others certified in the first round and left. She returned to her home and I returned to mine, but we have remained in touch to this day. I was hoping for a Merit Certificate, but when my final grades arrived in the mail, I learned I had missed it by one grade. We were all given a big project, a detailed scrapbook of business forms and letters that we worked on for the better part of the year. Unfortunately mine did not meet their standard, and I was given a C, which destroyed any chance of a Merit Certificate.

When I got home I told my mother I thought I might take the summer off. Yeah, right. She said I would do no such thing and to get busy going on job interviews. Oh well, it was a nice thought, but, of course, she was right. I accepted a job at the local university working as a secretary for three professors. My professional life had begun.

I was still dating the graduate student who had taken me to the spring formal at the Waldorf but after I was home for a few weeks, he returned to his country to spend the summer with his family. I was alone and vulnerable. And then it happened. One of the three professors I worked for was a young married man with an eye for the ladies. He was in his early 30s and soon made it very clear he found me attractive and desirable. I was flattered by his interest in me. We would steal a kiss in his office and sometimes I would return to the campus at night where we would meet for an hour or so and he would tell me how much he loved me. I was smitten. By the time my boyfriend returned to resume his studies in September, I was totally involved with the professor and broke off our relationship. He was crushed but I never looked back.

A few months after starting my first job, I won a small beauty contest and was crowned Miss Jaycee or Miss Junior Chamber of Commerce. That led to a chance to participate in a Miss America Preliminary Contest. The winner would go on to compete in the Miss New York State contest. The Jaycee's appointed a young man in their organization to be my escort. The escort's job was to make sure the contestant had everything she needed and to get her safely to the various events and rehearsals. He was a personable young man who had his own plane and one time invited me to fly with him to a nearby city for dinner. After awhile he wanted to be more than my escort and bought me a ring with my birthstone and called it a pre-engagement ring. I was horrified. I was not the least bit interested in him. Why would I be? He was reliable and polite and boring. He broke down in sobs when I told him after the pageant that I was not interested in continuing a relationship him.

How could I go out with him? I was in love with my young professor. Even though weeks earlier my supervisor had called me into her office and admonished me for having an affair with my boss and cautioned me against continuing with such inappropriate behavior, I was in love and didn't want to let go. Finally though, I decided the sneaking around and deception wasn't worth it and I changed jobs and moved to another department at the university. A few weeks later I learned that he was pursuing another young secretary.

After that I began dating some of the university students. I had a fun single life that included bowling once a week in the Women's Bowling League. I was a terrible bowler but it was a fun night of eating greasy hamburgers and French fries with the other women before we bowled. I also joined a social sorority that introduced me to some wonderful women and included activities such as fashion shows, conventions, and social get-togethers. I also enjoyed hanging out with my best friend Carolyn during our after work hours and weekends. My Willow Glen friends had gone off to college and scattered by this time so I lost touch with them. Carolyn and I were in sorority together and we both worked as secretaries during the week so we had a lot in common. As a result we spent all of our spare time with each other.

Eventually I entered into a serious relationship with a blue-eyed, red headed graduate student named Don. I adored him. We would spend hours in his private dorm room drinking wine and listening to Frank Sinatra records. Then he moved to an apartment with a terrific roommate and we had great times hanging out with our friends. He took me to Canada one weekend to attend a Shakespeare Festival. We had the best time wandering down quaint little streets and eating at outdoor cafes. He also accompanied me to New Jersey to attend the wedding of one of my friends from business school. But after a little over a year of very steady dating, he decided to break up with me one summer "to find himself." I was crushed. By fall the tears had pretty much subsided, but I was still feeling empty, lost, and lonely. I was living at home with my parents and occasionally my father would hint that he would like to me move out by asking, "When are you getting married?" I was in my 20s, and apparently he thought I was fast becoming an old maid. Then one day the phone rang. I answered and heard a deep voice say, "Hi Cat" – my heart fluttered in my chest. Only one person called me "Cat." Everyone else called me Cathryn. Jeff Wood was back.

We began to date, again, and before long we decided to get married. I was 22 and he was 23. We picked a date in August of 1965 for our wedding day. Don caught wind of my engagement and called and begged me not to marry Jeff but, of course, my mind was made up. Besides, where had he been all the time I was grieving over our broken relationship? By now I was head-over-heels in love with Jeff. If I hadn't been so blinded by love, I would have seen the red flags: (1) *He was unreliable.* On a few occasions Jeff failed to show up for our date. (2) *He was financially unstable.* He was in debt. He couldn't afford my engagement ring so I bought it, and he paid me back. (3) *He was a quitter and didn't finish what he started.* He quit high school just a few weeks shy of graduation over some petty issue and later got his GED while in the Navy. (4) *He was dishonest and sneaky.* He was dishonorably discharged from the Navy for breaking a serious rule. (5) *He didn't have a career or a career goal.* He didn't have much of a job. He was a clerk in the grocery store where his brother was the meat manager.

But his charm was all I could see, and charming he was. He was terribly romantic and would play the piano and sing to me on the nights we slipped into an intimate chapel on the university campus. We would go for romantic walks hand in hand. He knew just how to make me feel special, and I thought I was the most important person in the world to him. I had a beautiful, fairy tale wedding of white lace and promises which eventually turned into a life of turmoil and chaos. Gone were my carefree, single days.

Chapter 2

Married Life Begins

After our honeymoon at a little cabin owned by a friend of my mother's, we came home to our small one-bedroom apartment where I returned to work at the university and he returned to work at the grocery store. I was in love and SO happy. The only blemish in our relationship came about when I discovered my new husband was into pornography. I had no idea and was horrified when I discovered a stash of filthy magazines. Although I angrily confronted him, I eventually discovered he never gave it up.

About two or three months after we were married, he got a job as assistant manager at a larger grocery store in a city 90 miles away. I quit my job and we moved to another little apartment. This new life was a bit of an adjustment because he went to work in the afternoon and worked until well after the store closed at 10 p.m. I lived his schedule with him and would go to the store after it closed to help with whatever needed to be done. We would get home around midnight and then sleep late the next morning. However, I found that living his schedule didn't work well for me, plus we needed more income so I eventually went to work as a substitute secretary at nearby college. I enjoyed being back in the college setting. In the meantime, my husband's first of many affairs was brewing in our marriage, and we hadn't even been married a year yet. Her name was Annie, and she was a bookkeeper at the store. She came up to me at the staff Christmas party and told me to get lost because my husband didn't need a loser like me....or words to that effect. When I tearfully told Jeff what she had said to me, he laughed it off and basically told me to get over it.

Since we didn't have money to buy Christmas gifts for family members, I taught myself to make several different kinds of fancy bread and gave loaves of bread for gifts that year. It was a labor of love. I would have several batches going at the same time as I went around my living room punching down the dough so it could rise back up and then bake. I made four or five different fancy breads and they were so delicious. In February I entertained my parents and brother by fixing a turkey dinner. We didn't have a dining room so I set up a card table in the middle of the living room. My brother was astounded I had managed to fix an entire meal by myself. "You made this?" he said with surprise in his voice. In August, we celebrated our first anniversary by going out to dinner. By this time I was two months pregnant with my first child.

In November, Jeff informed me he had accepted a job as a store manager in Richmond, VA. In thinking back, I find it interesting that he never discussed any of this with me, just told me we were moving. So, we packed up what we owned in a U-Haul truck and my VW and drove to Richmond. We stayed at a motel, but money was tight so I cooked our breakfast in the bathroom using an electric frying pan. I cooked in the bathroom because of the ceiling fan that would suck up the smoke from my cooking. We found an unfurnished apartment in a big apartment building. The problem was the only furniture we owned was a bed. Some very friendly neighbors across the hall noticed our plight and loaned us a kitchen table and two chairs for the kitchen and a couple of folding lawn chairs to sit on in the living room. By now I was five months pregnant. I got a job answering phones in the office at a major department store.

After we had lived in Richmond for about three months, we had enough money to buy some furniture. Instead of buying furniture from a furniture store, we had a couch and two chairs custom made. Unfortunately they did not arrive until after our baby was born. However, the baby's room was furnished, and at night when I couldn't sleep, I would go in there and just look around in anxious anticipation of putting my baby to bed in the crib. Jeff would pick me up from work each night when he left the store. One night towards the end of my pregnancy, after I had walked down the center aisle the entire length of the rather large store to where Jeff was waiting for me at the front door, I was surprised when I got in the car and he gave me a big grin. I said "What?" and he said that he had enjoyed watching me waddle towards the car. We both laughed.

Cathryn M. Scott

In March, I gave birth to our first baby. Jeff came home from work to find me lying on the floor in our bare apartment dealing with the beginnings of labor. He took me to the hospital and was told to go back home. They would call him when the baby was born. I had such severe back labor pains that I couldn't tolerate it. The room was dark, I felt alone, and I was scared to death. Actually I was in a room with several other women in labor. A doctor came to visit the woman in the next bed and apologized for her discomfort and said he would get something for her. WHAT??? There's something for *discomfort???* I started to demand to be put out, and apparently I got what I asked for because the next thing I remembered was opening my eyes in a fog and seeing a beaming nurse holding a baby all wrapped up in a blanket in front of me. I then passed out again. Next I remember someone touching me, which was terribly annoying, so I kept pushing the hand away. Turns out it was Jeff who said he was trying to hold my hand but eventually decided the heck with me and went to see his daughter. Finally I emerged from the anesthesia and was delighted to meet my daughter for the first time. We decided to call her Stacey. The nurses all raved over her red hair, but I insisted it was just strawberry blonde. After all, we didn't have any redheads in our family, did we? Well, it turns out my mother's father did in fact have red hair. My grandmother was practically speechless when she met her Stacey for the first time and saw the red hair. I can still picture her as her jaw dropped and she turned to my mother and said with an incredulous look on her face, "She has red hair!!" My mother smiled and nodded. Oh how the past can come back to haunt us when we least expect it.

Sometime in late March our furniture arrived and in April my father came to meet his new granddaughter. He was the most animated I had ever seen him. He was so thrilled with her. It turned out that my father had a real weakness for babies and adored them. (Hope he doesn't mind me saying he adored something.) However, once a grandchild began to talk and have a mind of its own, he was done.

I've often wondered if the early bonding we were denied might have been the cause of his detachment. I am told that when they brought me home from the hospital, his draft notice from the Navy was in the mailbox. We were in the middle of World War II and he was sent away shortly after I was born and didn't return until I was two years old. My mother said he was different after he returned from the war and he refused to discuss what he had experienced.

But he actually laughed and cuddled with all of his grandchildren when they were babies. He turned out to be the only grandparent who came to see our baby. My mother said she couldn't get away from the office. And although I had a good relationship with Jeff's parents, for some reason they never came to visit us either.

After living in Richmond for about 6 months, Jeff gave me the good news that we were moving back "home" because he had landed a new job in our hometown. I was terribly homesick so I was beyond excited. Besides, life was beginning to unravel in Richmond. I was a stay-at-home mom and he was coming home drunk more and more often. Perhaps the newness of fatherhood had worn off and the burden of supporting a family was wearing on him. I don't know. All I know is we were very unhappy. He was never one to plod along day after day doing the same thing for any extended period of time. But I was hopeful that this change would put the marriage back on track.

Once again my little VW followed the U-Haul truck down the highway, only this time I had a sleeping baby in the back seat. There were no car seats in those days. I can still picture her sleeping on her tummy with her butt in the air in her car bed that lifted out of her carriage.

I was anxious to get back home for another reason. My mother had yet to meet her first grandchild and Stacey was three months old already. As soon as they met, my mother fell in love with her.

My parents ended up telling us about a new housing development that was under construction a few miles away, so we checked it out and were really impressed with what we learned. We signed a contract to have a little ranch-style house built to our own design and specifications. It would be ready in just a few short months. In the meantime we moved in with my parents. I can't remember where Jeff was working, but in the morning he would leave for work, and so would my parents, while I happily took care of Stacey all day. However, it wasn't long before my mother said I should put her in daycare and go back to work to help my husband support the family. Reluctantly I got a job as a secretary at the university, but I hated to leave Stacey all day every day. My mother told us about a woman named Mrs. Cummings who had a daycare in her home. My mother said she came highly recommended and was fussy about whose children she took, so she told Jeff and me to make a good impression on her when we went for our interview. We passed inspection and Stacey began to attend her daycare while I returned to work. I cried all the way to work the first day.

Living with my parents turned out to be a big mistake. Jeff hated it and began to stay out later and later and eventually came back to our bedroom quite drunk. One night my mother and I went out in search of him and found him in a bar. I asked her to drop me off so I could talk to him. He took me on a crazy and frightening ride through the streets of town and scared me so much I felt sick and screamed at him to stop the car. He yelled at me to shut up and stop being such a dramatic baby. I immediately had an attack of the dry heaves, but he wouldn't stop the car. Since living under such conditions was intolerable for all of us, by late fall I had found an inexpensive apartment for us to live in.

Although life didn't really improve, at least it wasn't being played out in front of my parents. I would pick up Stacey after work and she would be groggy and sleepy. I gave her some dinner, put her to bed, and stared out the window as I waited and waited and waited to see if or when Jeff would come home. On the weekends I did housework and took care of Stacey. I remember one time I was ironing while she was crawling around the ironing board. I looked down at her and realized I had no idea what to do with her. Since I spent most of my time at work now and very little time with her anymore, I felt as if I no longer knew my own child. I had no idea what to do with or for her beyond meeting her basic needs. Plus, I spent very little time giving her the attention she needed and deserved because I was so stressed over the fact Jeff was out drinking all the time.

One time he came home drunk and our car had a big slash in the hood. He had run into a sign. It had bent in half and sliced right through the metal.

In the spring our brand new little house was done and we were able to move in. Hopefully, a new beginning would take place. I was always optimistic things could change. Stacey was now a year old. For awhile things were good. She continued to go to Mrs. Cummings' daycare and I went to work and so did Jeff. Once again, I can't remember where he was working at this point because he was forever changing jobs. Our new house came completely furnished. Although we had our own living room furniture from Richmond, all of the rest of the house was completely and newly furnished. It even included a new washer and dryer in the basement. We were located in a really nice housing development that was growing steadily as new people moved in. Jeff planted grass. My grandfather gave me his gorgeous and meticulously pruned hedges to plant across the front of our property. I was delighted to have an opportunity to keep his hedges going for him since my grandfather had just learned he had to move out of his home. He and his fellow neighbors and been told they had to move out because all of the homes in his neighborhood were being torn down for a low income housing project. I was heartbroken for him and his elderly neighbors, all of whom had taken such pride in their homes.

We attended social functions with my sorority sisters and their husbands, we watched TV together at night, and we enjoyed family type activities. We were both gainfully employed and life seemed to be going in an orderly direction finally. I was happy.

As usual with Jeff, things could run smoothly for only so long before he became bored. I also think that since we seemed to always be short on money he didn't know how else to handle the stress other than to run away from it. He began staying out and drinking. One time I planned a surprise birthday dinner for him and invited my parents but he never came home that night. Another night I was sitting at the kitchen table typing a thesis for a graduate student to earn extra money when he came home drunk as usual and started showing me the frozen steak and lobster he had stolen from the freezer of a restaurant he had been drinking in that night. I looked at him disgustedly and said, "Wow, the great provider." He went ballistic and started throwing the frozen meat at me.

I finally couldn't take it anymore. I was getting scared he was going to hurt me. One night my parents and a couple of sorority sisters helped me to gather essential items for Stacey and me and then to put all the items in their cars. He was playing in a band by then so I knew he'd be out late. I have a vivid picture in my mind of two-and-a-half-year old Stacey sitting on my father's lap in a chair by the front door as things were being carried out, and at one point she pointed and said, "There's my toy box!" and my father quietly responded, "Yes, there it is." I left Jeff a detailed note so that when he came home to a partially empty house, he would know why. I was sad to leave my cute little house and all of the nice furnishings along with my dreams for a happily-ever-after, but it was clear there was not going to be a happily-ever-after the way things were going. Stacey and I moved in with my parents and for awhile I hid my VW behind their house in the backyard so he wouldn't see it when he came out to look for us.

After a few days, Jeff found out where we were and demanded to spend some time with his daughter. We never got a legal separation or arranged for court-ordered visitation, but he did spend some time occasionally with her before he moved to Florida to make it big as a singer.

I was content living at home with my parents and going to work every day. However, my father apparently was not happy with the arrangement. One day I was in the basement doing laundry when he asked me how much longer I planned to stay with them. Assuming he and my mother had discussed this and they wanted me to move out, I immediately began to look for a place for Stacey and me to live. Years later my mother overheard me telling this story to someone and she was completely shocked. She had no idea my father had essentially asked me to leave. She thought I had left on my own and I thought she wanted us to move out.

I found an inexpensive little two-bedroom trailer several miles outside town. It had a gorgeous big yard though with lots of tall mature trees. It was perfect for the two of us. We decided to get a cat so we went to the SPCA and walked past a few cages. We didn't get very far before a savvy black cat reached his paw out and grabbed Stacey's coat. Right then we knew he was ours. We named him Woody because our last name was Wood.

By this time I had changed her daycare from Mrs. Cummings, who we later determined was possibly abusing her and perhaps even drugging her which is why she was so groggy when I picked her up from daycare. By the time she was two, she would scream and put up a terrible fight when I went to drop her off. I figured she was just going through a phase so I didn't even think of changing to another day care. Besides, Mrs. Cummings was a large formidable woman and I was intimidated by her. However, by the time Stacey and I moved to the trailer in November of 1969, I knew it was time to remove her from Mrs. Cummings' care. Since I now drove past another day care every day on my way to work, I explained to Mrs. Cummings that it made more sense to change her to this more convenient location instead of going out of my way into town to take her to Mrs. Cummings' house. It turned out to be one of the best decisions I ever made. Stacey adored Miss Green and blossomed in her loving care.

Life in the trailer was difficult at best. I often didn't have enough money to feed us and so we frequently had dinner at my parents' house. Although there was a washing machine in the bathroom, there was no dryer, so I had to drape sheets, towels, clothes, etc. over a wooden drying rack that I set up inside the bathtub.

I was very lonely and scared. Then one day just before Christmas I got a call from Jeff, who was still living in Florida but his plans to make it big as a singer hadn't worked out. We decided to get back together and try again. I could not wait to see him. As usual, I was hoping for a new beginning. The night he walked into my trailer, he gave me the most passionate kiss I've ever had. Life was great and I fell in love with him all over again. Almost immediately I became pregnant with our son. I have a favorite memory of those early days when we were starting over. For a brief period of time, Jeff drove me to work so he could have the car for the day. Before reaching my office we would drop Stacey off at her daycare. The best part of those mornings was when Jeff would encourage her to sing "Puff, the Magic Dragon" with him as we drove down the highway. At times he could be such a terrific father.

I continued to work days at the university while Jeff smoked pot and made ceramics and played cards with his other unemployed friends during the day. There was a brief period of time when Jeff had a laborers' job at a company near our home, but he didn't stay there very long. Blue collar work wasn't for him. I would work all day, pick up Stacey from Miss Green's, and then come home and take off my work clothes and change into my hippy clothes. I was trying to be a free spirit like he was and actually found it fun for a time.

Soon Jeff had met another couple named Betty and Frank who were a bit older than we were but who shared his love of music, and they decided to form a little country band. Jeff told me I had to learn how to play drums. One of his drummer friends came to our trailer and taught me how to master a basic and very simple country beat. We practiced by pounding the couch with two drumsticks. Betty played bass guitar, her husband Frank played rhythm guitar, and Jeff played guitar and did most of the singing and interacting with the audience. We each had to join the local Musicians' Union so that our band could perform at various private clubs and jamborees. I was a terrible drummer but most of the time was able to keep a steady rhythm for the singers. Betty made our matching outfits – white shirts with green brocade vests and black string ties. She was about to start cutting material and sewing when I found out I was pregnant so she altered my vest to accommodate what was to come. I worked all week at my day job and played in the band in the evening on weekends.

With an expanding family, Jeff and I moved a couple of miles down the road from the trailer into a big old farm house that also had an apartment upstairs where two very nice male university students lived. We had three bedrooms, a bathroom, a large living room, a music room with a piano, an eat-in kitchen, and a room that could have been a dining room but we used it as just an empty room for Stacey to run around in. It also had a huge yard and a garage. Whenever I drove toward our house, I could hear one of John Denver's songs going through my mind .... "Country road, take me home, to the place I belong......." I was very happy there and it was so spacious after the cramped trailer. I also loved having a washing machine and a dryer. Another plus was the fact Betty and Frank lived within walking distance and their teenage daughter became our babysitter on the nights the band had a job.

I continued to work right up to the time of Andy's birth in August 1971. It became increasingly difficult to work all week and then play in the band on weekends. By the end of the night my ankles would be terribly swollen and I was exhausted. I could barely walk or hit the pedal on the bass drum. But if the people we were entertaining asked us to stay an extra hour, no amount of begging on my part to go home was heard. Jeff called me a whiner and a complainer, so I had no choice but to keep slapping those drumsticks until the others were ready to call it a night. The band ended its brief career a few weeks prior to Andy's birth, but before my membership in the local Musicians' Union expired, I had the notable distinction of being the only pregnant drummer in the union.

The weekend that Andy was born I painted our kitchen. I remember asking the doctor on Friday if I could and he said, "Yes, but you'd better hurry." By Sunday night I was in labor, so I was frantically folding laundry to get that job out of the way before I went to the hospital for a few days. This time when Jeff and I got to the hospital they didn't tell him to go home, and he was allowed to sit in a waiting room for expectant fathers. I was in much better physical condition this time because I had been much more active during the pregnancy. As soon as my precious baby was born they handed me a phone to call Jeff in the waiting room and I told him we had a son. My mother came to visit me in the hospital, which made me happy as well as surprised because she was very upset with me when I went back with Jeff and she and Jeff could not stand each other. She said he was nothing but scum and will never change and that I should get a divorce. I was hoping that she was wrong. After she had been visiting with me for awhile, Jeff appeared in the door of my room, saw my mother sitting there, and walked away. My mother smiled and said perhaps she would leave now so that Jeff could come in. I wished we could all get along but it just wasn't to be.

We had about two months that were quite pleasant. Jeff was now working as a salesman for a portrait company. I wrote in my journal that he was finally supporting his family and that I had a tuna casserole in the oven for that night's dinner and had baked a batch of brownies. I was happy and content in our farm house. Andy was a really good baby and always woke up with a smile.

But then things changed again. Jeff was never happy when things went along the same day after day.

This time it was because Jeff missed playing in a band and decided to help create a new one. My brother, who had been playing drums since he was a teenager, joined the band as their drummer. It was a band of several young men and one young woman named Sandy. They ended up with a weekly gig every Saturday night at a favorite night spot called Duncan's. And for awhile it was great fun. Every Saturday night all of the band spouses (Sandy's husband Troy was the only male in our group) would sit together at a table and enjoy the music and socialize. Afterwards we all went out for breakfast at a local diner. Betty and Frank's teenage daughter babysat every Saturday night.

When the band would practice at Sandy and Troy's house, I went with Jeff a couple of times, taking Stacey and Andy too, of course, but it soon became too difficult to remove them from their routine, so I stopped accompanying him after awhile. But I liked Sandy and thought she and Troy were a terrific couple. They had married really young – right out of high school. But he was a hard worker and they had a beautiful home, four young kids, a nice car, money to spend, and what was to me the perfect life. I was so envious since I had nothing close to that. She was a Day Care Mother and took care of kids all week, which added handsomely to the family income. I marveled at her ability to do that since being surrounded all day by little kids wasn't my idea of fun. I preferred working in an office. She had a fantastic voice and worked hard at being the group's female vocalist. But soon Troy and I began to notice Jeff and Sandy openly flirting with each other when they were singing on stage. It went beyond showmanship. This is what I wrote in my journal:

> "During this time my life became an impossible nightmare I couldn't escape. Every morning around 9 or 10:00 Jeff would leave for work as a salesman. He would return anywhere from 2-4 a.m., fall asleep on the couch or in bed, and then repeat it all again the next day. During the day

I took care of Stacey and Andy, drank coffee, smoked cigarettes, and stared out the window – endlessly. I lost a great deal of weight and became very listless. I had no car, no neighbors, no money. I went to the grocery store every Monday and went to Duncan's every Saturday night. I was sinking into a state of depression so the rest of the time I stared out the window wondering what was happening to my life. October, November, December day after long day. My life was crumbling around me.

"I remember one day as I sat in my chair by the window, it was winter, and the driveway had a lot of tracks in the snow from where the boys in the upstairs apartment had come and gone to the university a few times that day and perhaps Jeff's tracks as he drove away were left in the driveway. Stacey came to look out the window with me and as she looked at the driveway, she said, "Look at the tangled tracks." I felt so isolated – tracks left by people in cars going somewhere, while we remained constant prisoners in that house. By January we were so poor we had to go on welfare. In fact, they had to issue us an emergency check that first day we applied because we had no food in the house. I had no pride left – only an urgent need to feed my children.

"The winter continued. Bad storms prevented Jeff from coming home a few times. Once Sandy's father (who lived nearby and who, along with Sandy's mother, could see what was happening) brought me some groceries during a bad snow storm while Jeff stayed in town at his parents' house. I used to marvel at the fact that Stacey woke up eagerly each day even though we went nowhere, saw no one, did nothing. I never felt like playing with her because I was so desperately unhappy. I couldn't get over the fact she actually looked forward to each day. I couldn't understand why.

"January, February passed. By now it was obvious Jeff and Sandy were having an affair but nothing was out in the open yet. He loved to torment me though. One time he showed me pictures that had been taken of the band and pointed to Sandy and made a comment along the lines of 'Isn't she fantastic? Don't you think she's beautiful?' and then he'd put his face in mine and give me an evil sneer while I teared up and cowered. My birthday – Jeff promised to come home and take me out to dinner. I was turning 29. He didn't come home, of course. Sandy probably. The following night, 2/16/72, we went for dinner at Duncan's and he told me he was in love with Sandy. Some birthday. I knew it but to hear it really made me feel sick. He said he would stay with me until our bills were paid and we could afford a car for me. By this time our phone had been disconnected because his frequent calls to Sandy were long distance and the tolls added up quickly. I was totally alone and alienated from my own family.

"March 9, 1972. Stacey turned five. I had a party for her in the evening and invited my parents, the students upstairs, Jennifer [my brother's wife] and my two nephews, and my Saturday night babysitter. Jeff was going to be home for her party. He never made it. In fact, he didn't come home until 8 or 9 a.m. the next day. I found out later he'd spent the night at a motel because Sandy was able to be with him during the early part of the evening on the pretense of going to a Day Care Mothers meeting. After she went home he spent the rest of the night at the motel. He gave Stacey a card that morning when he came home. I was so mad I could hardly stand it.

"Shortly after that I refused to even go to Duncan's to watch him and Sandy make fools of themselves on the stage as they sang to each other. I asked his younger brother, Jake, to take me somewhere – anywhere – Saturday, March 18, 1972. I don't remember where we went but that night I talked and talked to Jake and really felt better by the time he took me home. Meanwhile Jeff was at Duncan's telling everyone I was cheating on him by running off with his own brother. Sunday, March 19, was a beautiful sunny day promising spring. I felt better after talking with Jake the night before and asked Jeff if we could go for a Sunday ride with the kids. Usually he spent every Sunday at Sandy's parents' home because Sandy, Troy, and the kids were there. He was **never** home. However, he packed our car with his clothes and said he was leaving me. I had put Stacey down for a nap so he went in to say good-bye. By the time he left, she was sobbing, and I was sitting in the kitchen feeding seven month old Andy. Out he walked. Shut the door. Drove away. I had no car, no phone, no money, no job, an innocent baby, and a sobbing five year old. Now what?"

The next few days were a total nightmare. I was paralyzed with fear and didn't know how I could go on. When I crawled into bed at night, I kept my arms and legs close to my body, afraid to stretch out and be reminded by the empty bed that I was now alone. On that Sunday morning he left, there was a smell of spring in the air and the day held promise of yet another new beginning. I was always hoping for new beginnings. I had no idea my world was going to come crashing down around me, and I didn't know how I was going to go on or if I even could.

A few days after Jeff left, Sandy announced to Troy that she wanted a divorce because she was in love with Jeff. He was just as devastated as I was and asked me if I had known this was happening. I told him I knew because Jeff had just left me and the kids. Troy loved his wife and their four children and worked hard to provide for them. He couldn't believe she was throwing it all away. Our family members and the other members of the band were shocked, angry, and disgusted. For the next several months, Troy and I gave each other strength and support as our spouses filed for divorce and made plans to marry each other. Our children were confused and upset by the way their lives had been turned upside down, so we spent much of the summer trying to make it better by taking them on fun outings. Fortunately they all enjoyed playing together. Troy planted a garden in my spacious side yard and showed me how to take care of it. He hung a tire swing from a big oak tree in the front yard so our children could play when we all got together.

In July we were both divorced and Jeff and Sandy got married. By September, I had really fallen for Troy and wanted us to stay together. He was everything Jeff wasn't, and I felt safe and whole once again. However, he met a young woman at work that he was now interested in. He said he couldn't stay with me because I reminded him of such a painful time in his life. Once again I felt as if I had been punched so hard I wasn't sure I could go on living.

In the fall we went our separate ways but not before my mother asked him to pick out a good car for me that she would pay for. In addition, my parents forked out around $2,000 to cover the outstanding bills I was left with so that I could start fresh. Now that I had my own car, I moved out of the country the first week in November and back to the city into a brand new apartment complex. Stacey was in kindergarten. I had resumed working at the university on October 2, 1972 in the Chemistry Department. I was 29 years old and starting over.

In the fall I was ordered to meet Jeff at the courthouse, which was located just a few blocks from the church in which we were married, to discuss child support. I had come from work so was dressed in business attire as I took my seat in the front row. The judge looked in the back row and said, "Who are you?" Sandy replied, "I am Mrs. Wood." The judge looked a bit disgusted. He then proceeded to ask Jeff about his financial situation and Jeff told him he was unemployed and had no income. The judge looked at me and asked me if I was aware of this and I dryly responded,

"*VERY.*" The judge then looked at Jeff and told him that as soon as he began to earn an income, he had to report it to the court so that proper child support could be determined. HA!!!! I knew that would never happen because Jeff had snarled at me on more than one occasion that he would go on welfare before he'd ever give me a dime. I never quite understood his animosity since he was the one who cheated on me and eventually walked away from his family. Jeff was one of the original dead-beat dads before the term had been invented.

It wasn't until after our divorce that I found out Jeff had always thought I was already pregnant with Andy when he came back to our marriage. The entire time we were married I had no idea he doubted his paternity because he never even hinted that's what he was thinking. After Sandy gave birth to a boy, I passed Jeff on the street one day and he sneered at me that he finally had a son. I told him over and over that blue-eyed Andy was his son but he would never believe me. This was before the days of DNA, but who needed DNA??? Years later an 18-year-old Andy was a handsome young man and an exact replica of his father at that age. Meanwhile, Stacey, who yearned to reconnect with the father who had abandoned her years before, searched for and found him when she became an adult. She soon discovered that her father refused to believe Andy was his child and this infuriated her. Finally one day she showed him Andy's high school senior picture. It was at that moment he realized he was wrong. Andy was clearly his son. He was a product of the Wood family without a doubt. All of the Wood males look surprisingly alike. He even resembles his half brother who was born to Sandy. Ooops. Jeff was really sorry. He asked Stacey if he could meet Andy. When Stacey told Andy she had found their father and he would like to meet him, Andy's response was an angry *"Hell no!"* He said he didn't want anything to do with a man who would abandon his wife and children and leave them to fend for themselves. Andy is now 40 and they have not met to this day.

Chapter 3

This Isn't What I Expected Of Life

I did not expect my life to be heading in this direction. Never did I think I'd be divorced and supporting two children on my own. Back in those days we weren't known as single parents. We were labeled "divorcees" and that sent up flags to other women to hold onto their husbands!! Divorce was not nearly as prevalent then as it is now and divorcees did not receive the sympathy and support that single parents do today.

One night I went to Stacey's school for a parent-teacher conference when she was in first grade and the teacher said to me, "Stacey does very well when we talk about families." I must have looked at her with a confused expression on my face because she went on to explain that they "read stories about families and she handles that quite well." I said nothing to the teacher but I went home seething with anger. Just because we didn't have a daddy in our house didn't mean we were not a family. Of course she understands "families" – she lived in one!!

Although my parents' marriage lacked the element called love, my brother and I had two parents in the home who together provided a stable environment. Both of my parents went to work every day and we were fortunate to grow up in a comfortable middle class family. My father built a modest 3 bedroom ranch-style house for us to live in complete with a finished basement with heated floors. They had a terrible marriage but they stayed married anyway. Every day my father came home from work and immediately descended the stairs to the basement where he had a little sitting area arranged in a dark back corner complete with a TV, recliner, and TV tray. He'd come upstairs for dinner and return for the rest of the evening to watch TV in what my mother called "his dungeon."

Obviously their situation was far from ideal but I didn't even have that much. My husband wasn't the least bit interested in providing a home or security for his family. He was completely self-centered. Several months after he left me, he came to visit me at my apartment and confessed he never gave it a thought what I would do when he walked out on me that day in March of 1972. He was still married to Sandy but things weren't going well. I got the feeling he was hoping I would reconcile with him but instead I told him that leaving me was the best thing he could have done for me. I learned they had violent arguments and Sandy accused him of cheating on her. One time, just before their marriage ended after 23 months, Jeff's mother told me that he had called her in the middle of the night and she could hear Sandy screaming at him in the background. He asked his mother if she would take care of their 10-month-old son, Jonathan, if anything happened.

When I returned to the university and began interviewing for a job, one prospective employer asked me if I planned to get married again. I told him I had no idea. He then said that I was young and attractive and would probably get married again so he didn't want to take the chance of hiring me and then have me leave. That conversation could never happen in today's workplace. Then I interviewed in the Chemistry Department and the climate was entirely different. After I was hired the professors for whom I worked made it clear that my role as a mother and my children came first and to never hesitate to stay home if one of them was sick. So I went to work in the Chemistry Department and began dating a series of professional university men. By the time I faced my first Christmas as a single parent I was dating a young chemistry professor named Warren. We had met at work and he was also recently divorced. We tried to help each other get through this emotional time. Afterwards I wrote the following entry in my journal:

"The kids and I had an enjoyable Christmas, but Christmas Eve was a little weird for me. Playing Santa Claus alone for the first time and all that. But I obviously lived through it, as I am discovering I manage to do through everything that happens to me. A few nights before Christmas and before Warren went to New York for the holidays, he came over and helped us put up and decorate the tree. After the kids were in bed, we settled down on the couch to look at the tree and listen to Christmas records. What a mistake that was! Both of us were feeling rather down and trying desperately to get into the spirit of the holidays. We thought that would help, but it didn't. I sat next to him on the couch and stared out the window and thought of Christmas Past. Apparently he was thinking of Christmas Past too because "Toyland" was playing on the record player and he said, 'I used to sing that to my daughter.' When I pictured this man tenderly singing "Toyland" to his tiny daughter at Christmas, I sat there and wept. I wept for all things that have gone wrong and wondered why. After awhile I sat up and announced that what we were doing was stupid and why didn't we turn off the records, turn on the radio, and see if the cinnamon-raisin bread I was baking was done yet. When I turned off the records and turned on the radio, Christmas music was on the radio! After I swore at the radio about its stupidity for playing Christmas music at this time of the year, we both began to laugh and to feel a little better. Besides, the bread was done and we sat there and finished almost one entire loaf of bread."

I had a busy social life but I didn't really like my job in the Chemistry Department. The work was not only boring, but I had to type complicated formulas that I didn't understand. Then I heard about a job as the Manager's Assistant at local major hotel chain. I interviewed for the job on April 30 and got it. I started my new job on Monday, May 21. I loved it but I sure was entering into unknown territory. I had never worked anywhere but the university. My boss' name was Quentin and we became very good friends. He was young and energetic and I really liked working for him. I also loved everything about the hotel business. First I was trained to run the switchboard. After that, they taught me how to use the special computer for making reservations in other hotels in our chain. From there I learned how to run the front desk and check people in. I was also expected to pitch in when the restaurant got busy by bussing tables. I would go home exhausted and aching from head to toe every night. It was totally different from working as a secretary at the university and I was loving every minute. I tried to absorb as much as I could as fast as I could.

On Friday, July 20, I had lunch with Quentin and a dentist friend named Logan Scott, Quentin's golf buddy. The next night Logan and I went out for dinner at a beautiful restaurant on the lake. The next month we went out a second time and then we began to date regularly. I had been dating several interesting men before I met him but in time I decided to just date Logan exclusively.

But in August my new world fell apart. On August 16 some company executives came in and fired Quentin. Then a 57-year-old man, who was now the new Manager, came to me and said, "You've done a fine job here and I want you to know this is nothing personal but I'm going to have to ask you to leave because I'd prefer to work with a girl I've worked with before and who knows me and my way of doing things." When I tearfully sobbed to him that I had two children to support, he patted my hand and assured me I'd find another job. But I had loved that one!!! I was home by lunch time in total shock and mad at the world. I called Logan to tell him what had happened and he suggested I take a vacation. That was a stupid thing to suggest because I needed to be looking for my next job but I decided to use my hotel connections and took the kids to Vermont for a few days. Believe me, I would have felt more rested had I gone looking for another job but the trip definitely took my mind off my troubles. We had a good time swimming in the motel pool and visiting Santa Land and other places of interest, but vacationing with two young children without another adult to help is not the best way to go. At the end of the trip we were driving home from our little vacation when I looked in the rear view mirror and saw Andy hanging practically upside down in his car seat eating his chewable vitamins as fast as he could. I was driving down a busy highway and couldn't pull over so I screamed at Stacey to stop him. Relaxing vacation....yeah, right.

When I returned home I began looking for another job at the university. I also began to see Logan with increasing regularity. I soon discovered he was a brilliant dentist but didn't know the first thing about taking care of himself. Enter the great al-anon. Al-anons are known for such qualities as needing to rescue and take care of others and be in charge whereas alcoholics are totally helpless and disorganized and have trouble doing the simplest task without creating a disaster. We were made for each other. I went to his apartment just once and was shocked to discover he had never gotten around to getting any furniture. The kitchen was a mess and the stove was splattered with grease from the hamburger he had fixed for his dinner the previous night, the only food he knew how to prepare.

I had two interviews at the university on September 26. I found out on the 28th that I was being offered a job in the administrative offices. I began on October 8. However, September brought another crisis. Logan started acting really weird. He was so strange that Quentin and I thought he was on drugs. He would leave his job to go to lunch and then never come back. He thought others were out to get him. He was just very very strange. We called his parents and they told us he had been diagnosed years earlier with paranoid schizophrenia and had obviously discontinued his required medication. Today it is called Bipolar Disorder. On September 25, I noted in my calendar that Logan left for Indiana where his parents lived to seek treatment. He was not able to return until October 31. By then he had lost his job in the dental practice where he had been employed.

Why did I continue to date him? Well, prior to his complete melt down, his condition wasn't evident much of the time because he was taking his meds.

Occasionally he would act a bit unusual but I dismissed it because he was usually so much fun. Plus he was warm and loving. He was intelligent yet had a great sense of humor. I had been dating a series of very interesting men but none of them really stole my heart. They were either highly intelligent but boring scientists or sports fanatics who couldn't talk about anything else. I dated a couple of other men who didn't fit either of those categories but nothing really clicked. Logan was a delightful combination of all of the men I had been seeing. At the end of October he returned to town in a much more stable frame of mind. He decided to buy his own dental practice instead of working for someone else. He bought a practice in a little village over 100 miles away that I had never heard of – Bonnyville. He assumed ownership in February and moved into the home of a lovely family with whom he had recently become friends. He would stay there during the week and then come to my apartment on the weekends.

We began a pleasant and very workable routine of going our separate ways during the work week and having family time with the kids on the weekends. Besides going to work every day, I spent my time going to sorority meetings a couple of nights a month and I was involved in Brownies and other activities that Stacey participated in. Our kid-friendly apartment complex had a Halloween celebration in the fall and watermelon parties in the summer. Stacey and Andy enjoyed playing with the other children and I appreciated the fact it was a safe environment for them to be in. The living room had sliding glass doors that led to a small grassy area behind our apartment. One time I was outside in this grassy area playing catch with Andy, who was around 3 at the time. A young mom came over to me and gave me the best compliment I could have ever gotten. She said I appeared to spend more quality time with my children than she did and she was a stay-at-home mom! As a busy and frequently exhausted divorced mom, I was never sure I was giving my children an adequate childhood so that was a big boost to my self-esteem.

After dating for a year, Logan and I began to talk about marriage. This turned into a big ordeal that should have alerted me right then and there to not pursue it any further. But I didn't listen to my instincts because I ultimately wanted to be a stay-at-home mom and have at least one more child. So I overlooked a lot of issues I should have paid attention to. For example, when we first brought up the thought of marriage, his parents, even though they had met me and said they liked me, told Logan they would disown him if he married me because I was a divorcee with two children *who might turn on him one day because he wasn't their real father.* Finally we were able to get their blessing.

But after that he began to upset me because he frequently found fault with me and belittled me. He badgered me about how I should be painting my finger nails and toe nails like other women. (I didn't want to bother.) He wanted me to learn how to cook better. (When did I have time to do that? I fixed a quick and simple meal every night for myself and my two very young children after I got home from a full day at work.) I was taking a college course at the university in the Women's Studies Department called "Women in America" and he criticized me for wasting my time on such a stupid and unimportant course.

He pointed out to me on several occasions that while he was pursuing a career as a dentist, I was getting married, having babies, and ultimately plummeting into a life of desperation when my income fell below the poverty level forcing me to request assistance from Social Services in order to survive. He was obviously implying that while he was becoming a success, I was living a life of failure. I would never tolerate anyone speaking to me like that today. But I was young and unsure of myself and having a man speak down to me wasn't as foreign and uncomfortable as it should have been. We spent the better part of 1975 waffling back and forth between getting married or just continuing our weekend arrangement.

We had a big argument and broke up for a week in September. During that time period I told my female supervisor at the university that we had broken up. She said she felt I could do better and that it was probably for the best. Logan and I had been dinner guests at her house on a couple of occasions so she had met him and told me she wasn't comfortable with the way he would put me down. I was surprised. She saw him put me down? When? She went on to recall an incident when we were talking about something at her house after dinner and Logan, referring to the subject they were discussing, waved his hand in my direction and made the remark "Cathryn doesn't know anything about this...." and she said she thought that was a rude thing to say. I thought that was interesting because I remembered the incident she was referring to and didn't think anything of it at the time because I figured he was right. Cathryn *doesn't* know anything......

However, at the end of the week following our big fight he returned and we went out for drinks. After much discussion, we decided to get married November 1. It was the end of September and we had a month to put together a wedding and buy a house in Bonnyville.

Chapter 4

Married Life Begins Again

October was a blur of wedding activities – got my dress, got the rings, got our marriage license, attended a surprise bridal shower given by my my sorority sisters, quit my job at the university, and had lunch with friends. If I had any doubts, it was too late now. I was pushing down all of the red flags because by now I was tired of going to work every day. I wanted to spend time with my children and perhaps have more. They were growing up fast and I was missing out on being with them as much as I would like, so I decided to give marriage another try. Another reason to try it? I remembered writing in my journal in August 1972, just as I was facing the reality that Jeff was gone and so was Troy and I now had to make some decisions about how to go on from there. I wrote:

"Summer is slipping into fall…I stare at the dandelions Stacey picked for me now floating wilted in a plastic cup of water and I pause before I throw them out – remembering the day she gave them to me – blue eyes sparkling – hand behind her back as she clutched the flowers – 'I have a surprise for you!' As I pick up the toys scattered thru the house I remember the noisy fun Stacey and Andy had playing with them. And I can still see Andy clumsily attempting to walk and then falling a few steps later. I'll miss these things when I return to work in a few weeks. But everything eventually comes to an end – the summer – and staying home all day."

On November 1, our wedding day arrived overcast and chilly. I had my hair done at 8:30 a.m. and at 1:00 I walked down the aisle of the Roman Catholic Church. Although I was Protestant, Logan insisted on being married in the Catholic Church. Fortunately I was allowed to have my own minister participate in the ceremony, which made me feel much better. My brother's wife was my matron of honor and Stacey and Andy preceded me down the aisle. Stacey wore a floor length flowered dress and had a wreath of flowers in her hair while Andy was wearing a suit and tie and sporting his first boutonniere. When the priest said "You may kiss the bride," Logan bent me backwards and caused a ripple of laughter throughout our friends who had come to witness our nuptials.

We had a small dinner at my parents' house following the ceremony. I went into the bathroom to freshen up and caught the reflection of my shiny new gold wedding band in the mirror and immediately thought: "What have I done?" It was only a fleeting thought that quickly disappeared and was replaced with a sense of confidence that I had made the right decision and everything would be fine.

By November 2 I was pretty sure I had made another mistake. While I cheerfully made light conversation while we drove to Canada for our honeymoon, he suddenly interrupted to remind me that he was very important because he was a doctor and I had just better take good care of him or he would get rid of me. It was all about how much he expected me to do for him. I was stunned and started crying. Get rid of me? I couldn't survive another divorce!! Meekly I promised him everything would be fine. The thought of being divorced a second time scared me and was far more than I imagined I could ever endure again. Years later it occurred to me that never once did the conversation include what his responsibilities as a husband just might be towards me. It was all about him. Our honeymoon was a dreadful experience with Logan wanting to sleep most of the time so I explored the gift shop and the nearby vicinity by myself. We cut our honeymoon short and headed for home.

I was glad to get back home and part company with him for a week. I picked up Stacey and Andy, who had stayed with my parents, and he went back to work in Bonnyville. I packed up my apartment all week (which included the living room furniture Jeff and I had bought in Virginia when Stacey was born), got my name changed on my license and registration, de-enrolled Stacey from school, and on Friday two young men Logan had hired arrived in a U-Haul from Bonnyville and loaded up my possessions. We were ready to go! My mom was coming with us and we were finally all set to leave our now empty apartment except for one thing! I couldn't find our cat, Woody. He had moved with me from the trailer to the farm house to my apartment and he did not want to move anymore! He saw the truck and watched stuff being carried out and took off for the woods in the back of the apartments. I called and called but he wouldn't come. Finally I dug out my electric can opener (this was before the days of lids that popped off), plugged it into a nearby outlet, stood on my back deck and turned on the can opener. Whirrrrr!! Sure enough, he came running – FOOD!!!! I grabbed him and shoved him into his cat carrier and off we went to Bonnyville and our new life.

I remember when we turned the corner from Maple Street onto Parker Street, there was Logan waiting outside in the yard with a big smile on his face. OK. Maybe this won't be so bad. I was once again looking forward to seeing him and pushing the bad honeymoon memories aside. Of course, I had told no one about my honeymoon nightmare so my mother assumed I was just thrilled to see my new husband after being apart for almost a week.

It was great fun getting settled in my own house. I hadn't had a house of my own since the little three bedroom ranch-style house Jeff and I had built in 1968 but eventually walked away from in 1970. After several years of living in an apartment, it was so nice not to have someone living on the other side of the wall and to be able to leave toys out in the yard and not be afraid someone would steal them. Logan and I had looked at a few other houses but I had fallen in love with this colonial-style home on a corner lot. It just said "home" to me. There were two bedrooms and a bathroom upstairs where Stacey and Andy had their rooms. Downstairs there were two more bedrooms, a full bath, a galley-style kitchen, a small dining area, and two living rooms with a fireplace in the first one. The second one Logan wanted to call the den, so that's what it was called. Beyond the kitchen was a small laundry room with stairs that led down to the basement and a door that led out to a partially enclosed back porch. The porch led to the attached two-car garage. There was a half-circular driveway in the front. Plus there was a quarter of an acre of land all around the house. It felt huge to me. We had all new carpets put in and we put up new wallpaper in Andy's room. We had several rooms painted and we hung curtains. I planted flowers, and the kids made friends with the other kids on the street. Even Woody loved exploring his new environment. It was a quiet, dead-end street and an ideal spot to raise children. Our yard became the neighborhood mecca for football games, tree climbing, camping out, basketball in the driveway outside the garage, and eventually hours of fun in our pool.

Because Logan was embarrassed over the fact I had been married before, he insisted the kids change their last names from Wood to Scott. Marrying someone who had been married before amounted to loser status for him. I can thank his parents for that point of view. For the first few years of our marriage, they simply *used* the name Scott, but eventually I had their names legally changed. They were never adopted because Logan's father advised him not to just in case they got into legal trouble when they got older and dragged him into it with them. I thought my children had been welcomed as members of the family and that even though I wasn't Catholic, the fact I was a good Christian was enough to warrant acceptance, but I was never totally forgiven by any of them for being divorced. I was instructed to forget I ever had a life before I knew Logan and many people in Bonnyville didn't know for several years that Stacey and Andy were not his biological children. Years later when I was packing up my possessions to move out of the house, I discovered he had gone down to our basement and gotten into my trunk where I kept several personal mementos and thrown out my wedding album from my first marriage.

Stacey enrolled in the local elementary school in third grade as Stacey Scott and I was so proud of the way she was able to change her name on her school papers. Andy was only four and just learning to write his name but one time he was sitting in the back seat of the car as we were all going somewhere and he was holding a box of wooden blocks. He innocently pointed to the word "Wood" on the side of the box and remarked, "That used to be our name." I quickly hushed him because something like that could cause Logan to explode in an instant. As it turned out, he either didn't hear him or wasn't paying any attention and I breathed a silent sigh of relief. I felt very lucky that they quickly adapted to calling him "Daddy."

In January I was delighted to learn I was pregnant. In March I registered Andy for kindergarten. Stacey joined Brownies and we began to become part of the community. I attended PTA meetings. In the summer the kids attended Vacation Bible School at the church we attended, and I began to make many nice friends. We had an active social life going out to dinner with several other couples almost every weekend or having friends over for dinner. But there was also a darker side. My new husband spent many nights going out drinking. The difference here was he always came home after work for dinner. I was becoming a really good cook now that I was home and had the time to prepare nice meals but he went out many nights by himself. The other difference was he wasn't cheating on me or looking for other women, but it made me mad that he went out so often. Usually he slept on his days off or he played golf. In the spring he bought a riding mower so that it would be easier for me to cut the grass since I was pregnant and he wanted to play golf.

In August our daughter Ashley was born. Stacey, who was now 9 ½ years old, was so excited to have a baby sister and practically became her surrogate mother. She carried Ashley on her hip for so many months that I wasn't sure Ashley would ever learn to walk. Andy, who had turned 5 two weeks after she was born, thought she was very nice but preferred to go out and play ball or dig holes in the dirt with his trucks. Logan was so joyfully ecstatic over the birth of his very own child that it triggered a change in his relationship with Stacey and Andy. The close father-daughter and father-son relationship that had developed over the last few years suddenly disappeared and he only cared about Ashley. No one could have seen this coming and had I known it would happen I would never have married him and put my children in such a precarious situation. But it's always so much easier to see things in hindsight.

I couldn't believe it the first time he seemed to enjoy seeing me struggle with the demands of motherhood. After the first day of school, Stacey came home with books that needed to be covered. Since the school did not provide book covers, we had to make our own out of paper grocery bags. It's not a hard job but requires both hands. Ashley was in her infant seat on the dining room table where Stacey and I were working on cutting out the paper bags and taping them to make book covers. Ashley was being fussy so I was trying to rock her in her little seat while helping Stacey. Suddenly Ashley's crying got louder. Logan came in from the den, drink in hand, and smirked at me while I struggled to multi-task and said, "Can't handle it, can you?" It never occurred to him to ask how he could help. He expected me to do it all and found it amusing when I couldn't.

This attitude of superiority was handed down from his father. His father would bark orders at Logan's mother and she would hurry around to wait on him. I overheard Logan bragging to his father one day on the phone that he had noticed something hadn't been dusted well and had told me I'd better start doing a better job! Of course, what he failed to also report was my response at the time which was, "If you don't like the dust, clean it yourself." No, it was just important that he made his father proud by showing him he was the boss in his home.

The holidays were Logan's favorite time of the year and he enjoyed Christmas with the enthusiasm of a small child. He bought colored lights to string in the little white birch tree by our front driveway. We had tall electric candles on the little front porch. Another tradition that delighted him was throwing ice cubes on the roof Christmas Eve after the kids had gone to bed. He would ring bells and throw ice cubes and then come bursting into the house loudly "whispering" that Santa was right outside. How were the kids expected to sleep with that going on? When we spent New Year's Eve at home, which was most of the time when the kids got a little older, I made our favorite snacks and we munched all evening. At midnight we all rang our noise makers and then Logan would go outside on the front porch and yell "Ring in the new!!!" That, of course, brought our neighbors out to wish us a Happy New Year as well.

Stacey joined Girl Scouts and began taking tap dance lessons. I became a Girl Scout leader and started a Cadette troop when the girls entered their teen years. One warm fall day as the new scouting year was just beginning, I was sitting outside on the grass talking with my Cadette troop about our plans for the coming year when one of them turned to me and said she was going to quit because it wasn't "fulfilling." I gulped and thought to myself, "Fulfilling? Excuse me?" I had no idea how to make the Girl Scout experience fulfilling. Oh dear, was I letting her and the others down? But the other girls didn't seem to share her opinion and enjoyed the activities I planned without any complaints of being unfulfilled.

When Andy became a Cub Scout, I became a Den Mother and then later Scout Master when there were no men willing to take the position. Cub Scouts were a little easier to make happy but a lot noisier that my Girl Scouts. I set up a work space for us in the basement by putting large pieces of plywood over saw horses. I borrowed folding chairs from my church. We spent many happy hours making crafts, playing games, and eating snacks. In the fall I took them on a hike up a mountain where our snack was apples. One time I had an ice cream eating contest which I should never have done. One little boy was so wildly competitive that he almost caused bodily harm to himself as he shoved the cold ice cream down his throat. Every year we held a Pinewood Derby where the boys and their dads were to work on the car together and then race it at a designated monthly meeting, which was held upstairs in the fire hall. In many cases the boys watched as their fathers trimmed and painted and decorated the cars and glued the weights on to make them fly down the track the fastest. When it came time for the race, the fathers and their sons came together to have their car weighed prior to the race. I was the person weighing the cars and one time a car weighed over the limit but when I mentioned this to the father, he went ballistic on me. He then stormed out to his car to get his own scale to prove to me that the car was within the proper weight. Although I told the father that all cars had to be weighed with the scale I was using, he got downright nasty so I backed down. After all, this was supposed to be a fun competition for the boys but the fathers took it personally. Logan helped Andy with his car and insisted on lots of pin striping because he loved pin striping.

But even though there were happy times, Logan's drinking slowly got worse and worse and I would have trouble getting him to take his required medication to treat his mental illness. Each year it got a little bit worse. People with his form of mental illness medicate themselves with alcohol and as a result rarely seem to get drunk. Sometimes he would wake me up in the middle of the night, grab my wrist to pull me out of bed out to the dining room table, and demand that I tell him how I think. Tell him how I think? What kind of question is that? Other times I would be watching TV and he would turn it off and demand that I talk to him. I would look at him and wait for him to begin a conversation but he expected me to talk. He got furious when I had nothing to say. If I didn't have the TV on but was reading a book, he would get angry and snatch it out of my hands and tell me to talk to him. Another time I saw him walking through the house with tissues hanging out of his ears. He looked like a lop-eared rabbit. I asked him why he had tissues in his ears. He replied, "So you won't hear the voices in my head."

I recall one night I was experimenting with a craft project for my Cub Scouts at the dining room table after dinner. I always tried out a craft before teaching it to the boys so I could ensure success. Logan walked by and asked me why I was wasting my time with such a stupid activity.

So, after a few years, I was glad when he went out and wasn't at home. Everyone was much more relaxed. The only way I could survive was to become more and more immersed in my children's activities and in activities of my own. I went camping with the Girl Scouts, I taught Sunday School and was involved in many other church-related activities. I went on field trips with the school. I joined a women's book club, went to a weekly Bible study, and attended Stacey's dance recitals.

It was assumed we had plenty of money since my husband was a doctor, but that wasn't the case. He was a terrible business person and had no idea how to handle money. He was incapable of considering the fact that bills had to be paid out of his income. He only saw the deposits that came in and would write checks to himself all the time so he could go out drinking or buy whatever else it was he wanted. Plus he felt the need to impress his wealthy out-of-town patients. After completing an expensive procedure on them, he would slap them on the back and tell them "No charge." His receptionist/bookkeeper finally came to me one day and said she quit because she could no longer stand the pressure of trying to pay the bills with what little money he left in the account. That meant I now had to step in and help out in the office.

Logan had several days when he would act erratically and although his patients were never in danger, several good patients decided to seek dental care elsewhere. He was lucky to always have competent dental staff hovering over him at all times. Plus he truly was a gifted dentist, so no one was ever harmed or mistreated, but I couldn't blame them for looking for someone else with whom they might feel more confident. As the income slowed down, he decided to open a second office back in my hometown. The original plan was to return there eventually because I had never fully embraced Bonnyville and wanted to move back home.

Logan's lack of business sense was demonstrated once again. He and I decided he should look for a practice to buy. After that we hoped we'd be able to sell the Bonnyville office and relocate the family. The proper procedure would have been for him to consult with his accountant after finding a practice he wanted to buy. His accountant would then advise him what to offer and work with him when it came to financing. But that's not what happened. After Logan found a practice that was for sale, he simply went ahead and bought it for the asking price. When his accountant found out, he was furious and screamed, "Why am I your accountant?" He quit working for him.

However, the papers were signed and it was too late to do anything about it. We had no choice but to move forward. We kept the dental hygienist who had worked for the previous dentist because she was wonderful at her job and knew all of the patients. Besides, I went to high school with her so I knew her as well. Then, with her help and suggestions, I interviewed and then hired a receptionist. Logan worked at the new office Mondays and Tuesdays, took Wednesday off, and then worked in his Bonnyville office Thursdays and Fridays. This worked out fine when he would take his medicine and go to work, but that wasn't always the case.

As the years went by, everything slowly deteriorated. The practices were in trouble. His staff had to cancel patients' appointments frequently because he would either not show up after lunch or would tell his staff to cancel his appointments. He would leave early in the new office or refuse to get out of bed when he was home. The marriage was all but over. He wouldn't take his medicine with any regularity and his mental state kept getting worse as a result. I was also angry because he openly favored Ashley by frequently bringing her gifts when he returned home after two days in the other office while Stacey and Andy stood by and watched empty handed. When I asked him if he had anything for them, he would search through his pockets and hand them a stick of gum. Ashley was too young to realize anything was amiss so I would attempt to make a joke of it with Stacey and Andy by laughing and telling them that Ashley got a new pair of roller skates because she did such a good job breathing. They would laugh with me as if we had a private joke from everyone else. Even though I spoke with him often about this unfair treatment, the gifts didn't stop. He had no idea how much he was hurting Stacey and Andy.

I had hired an accountant in Bonnyville and he eventually decided that the only way we could get Logan to stop writing checks to himself would be to remove the checkbook from him. He would now get a weekly allowance. Naturally this made Logan angry but there was no other way to keep him from spending the money before we could pay the bills that were now piling up at an alarming rate.

The next few years were a slow and painful emotional deterioration for me. He continued to fight me every morning when I brought him his pills. His mental stability was weakened as a result and I was getting run down trying to keep life normal for everyone. I kept busy with the many activities the kids and I were involved in while trying to keep him stable and reassure the staff in our two practices that all was fine. I was also trying to put on a brave face in the community. One example was my car. In 1977 Logan bought a brand new station wagon for me to drive thus finally replacing the car my mother and Troy had gotten for me. Now it was covered with rust and falling apart. One day the wife of one of our local attorneys said to Logan, "Why don't you buy your wife a new car?" I inwardly cringed because a new car was the last thing we could afford. We were struggling to keep our children clothed and fed and our bills paid. As I recall Logan simply turned and walked away rather than answer her question.

I began to take Logan to see a series of different counselors and doctors but he disliked all of them. I introduced him to my counselor and he disliked her as well and began to refuse to keep his appointments. I felt like a prisoner in my own life but had absolutely no idea how to escape. One day I was having lunch with his office manager in

Bonnyville and she asked me if I planned to live like this forever and I didn't have an answer. All I knew was that I was trusting God to take care of me somehow and someday.

Stacey graduated from high school in June of 1985 and, at my insistence, went to a nearby community college. She and her boyfriend didn't want to be apart so he enrolled too and went with her. I was not happy about this situation but there was nothing I could do about it. However, college was something she never wanted so she and her boyfriend quit after one semester. When she came home at the end of the semester she announced that they wanted to get married. Once again I disagreed with her decision, but it didn't matter. She was almost 19 years old and in love – I didn't have a chance.

There certainly was no money to spend on a wedding or a reception, so we made plans to have a tiny ceremony for the immediate family only in the church sanctuary. However, members of our church family heard about the impending marriage and our phone began to ring as people offered everything needed for a proper church wedding. It started with the offer of a wedding dress and veil. Stacey was thrilled. After that other offers were made. Flowers were donated and a wedding cake was made by one of our talented church women. The minister announced the time and date of the wedding in church and invited the congregation to attend. The entire ceremony got much bigger than I had anticipated or wanted. All I could do was thank everyone and allow them the fun of putting together our little wedding.

Wedding day in January of 1986 arrived with a big snow storm. Regardless, there were many of our church friends as well as my parents, my brother, and one of my nephews. Andy escorted me to my place in the front pew as the organist played. When the wedding march began, Logan proudly walked Stacey down the aisle and gave her away. We had a modest reception in the church basement consisting of wedding cake and punch. Afterwards, the newlyweds drove to their apartment in a nearby city using Logan's car because they didn't own one of their own. The next day we loaded my station wagon with their wedding gifts and delivered them to the happy couple. We then drove both of our cars home and left them on their own. At this point I had to let go and hope for the best because I now had some major problems of my own to cope with.

In February Logan began to spin out of control and was in a full crisis by the end of the first week. It began with heavy drinking and then cancelling patients followed by sleeping all day. I was in close touch with my counselor who was helping me deal with this turn of events. In my journal entries I referred to this time period as "L's crisis." One time I wrote that he woke me up shortly after I went to bed and began babbling that he was criminally insane. I never went back to bed that night. I called my counselor in the morning who said it was time to have him committed to a psychiatric ward in the hospital.

The State Police arrived at 10 a.m. on a Sunday morning and he went with them peacefully. I followed later and filled out the papers to have him committed. Once he was there, he made repeated collect calls to me that I refused to accept. However, he was medicated and released a week later. There were no changes in his behavior and I couldn't understand why he could come back home. I was now close to a complete mental breakdown. I had no idea how to get untangled from my life. I had no income of my own. If I were to leave him, he would stop working altogether and follow me. My personal sanity was being damaged as I struggled to separate what was normal from what was not.

However, as a result of the new medications he was receiving, by March our life was back to a reasonably normal routine of Logan working out of town on Monday and Tuesday and working in Bonnyville Thursday and Friday. He was seeing a new doctor in named Dr. Branson. After working with Logan for several sessions, Dr. Branson, who was at least in his late 60s or early 70s, told me he had never seen a more difficult or stubborn case. Logan hated Dr. Branson and fought me every time I took him for his appointment. At the end of April he refused to keep his appointment with Dr. Branson. Also, he was becoming a fire hazard. On a couple of occasions he left the tea kettle going on the stove and burned them both times. Another time he was taking care of Ashley while I was at a meeting. He put a candle on the back of the toilet so she could have a candlelight bath. What he failed to take into consideration was the fact the candle was underneath a towel hanging from the towel rack. The towel caught on fire and Ashley started to scream, which brought Logan running to put the fire out.

One day in May I took Andy and Ashley with me to see the new apartment Stacey and her husband had moved into. Leaving Logan alone in our house was always a bit of risk because he often got into "trouble." For example, he got rid of several of our family pets when the kids and I were out of the house. He took Ashley's favorite cat Martha (aka Marfa) out to the country and left her to fend for herself. He said he didn't want her around anymore. Another time I had taken the kids to the orthodontist 90 miles away and he called me on their office phone to tell me he had taken our dog to the SPCA. The only animal he never messed with was Woody, who died when Stacey was 16. He would rummage through my personal papers to read my journals or go through my personal items. This time while I was gone, Logan took it upon himself to call the accountant I had hired to handle our financial affairs. He was angry that this accountant refused to give him access to the checkbook so he could write checks whenever he wanted to. He demanded to have the checkbook and told the accountant he was fired. Then Logan called me at Stacey's apartment to tell me the accountant had quit. I was devastated. This was a man from my church that I trusted completely who had been doing a great job keeping us on top of our financial commitments. A few days later the accountant told me what had really happened so I felt better knowing he hadn't quit, but I was still very upset regardless.

I taught a women's Sunday School class that summer and the weekly lesson preparations kept me occupied. Plus Andy and Ashley's friends and activities also helped to keep my mind off the larger problems looming in my life. But I developed painful back spasms that took my breath away. At the end of the summer I finally saw a doctor and they were diagnosed as stress related. One day in June I told Logan that he was making me crazy so he picked up the phone and called Dr. Branson to make an appointment for *me*! At that point Dr. Branson changed Logan's medications and also prescribed a sleeping pill so he would sleep at night.

I wasn't the only one stressed to the limit. Logan's office staff had pretty much had it as well. He wanted to discontinue seeing Dr. Branson so he decided to shop for another doctor when he was working at his other practice. One day he went to see a doctor during his lunch hour. The doctor took away his car keys, gave him some Valium, and put him in a room at the Ramada Inn. He never returned to work for his afternoon patients and left his staff wondering where he was. That was the final straw. With Dr. Branson's blessing, along with that of my counselor, I instructed the women in the other office to quit their jobs. On a hot Monday morning in August of 1986 they told Logan they were done and that his patients had been told the practice was closing. They told him they simply couldn't handle it any longer. He came home angry and frustrated. Later that night he drove to a farm house outside the village where a couple named

Tom and Rita lived. They were well known in Bonnyville for welcoming people into their home who were struggling with alcohol and/or drug addiction and helped them get their lives back on track. Logan told them he had to get away from me because I was turning him into a drug addict by making him take drugs. Rita called me and told me what Logan told her. I explained that he suffered from schizophrenia and was required to take the medication I was giving him. She said she understood but under the circumstances she had no choice but to believe him and take him to a hospital in a nearby town in Pennsylvania and put him in detox. I said fine. I called my counselor and told her what had happened and she advised me not to let him back in the house once he was released. What? Not let him come home? Was I allowed to do that? She said I had every right because he was not going to get better if he came home and it would no doubt be my final undoing if we continued together.

Naturally over the course of the next few days he went totally out of control since he was taking no medication. A doctor was quickly called in to treat him. He was released from the detox unit of the hospital and told he was to begin seeing the doctor as an out-patient and get back on a regime of medication. When he called to tell me this, I told him he could not come home. Upset and angry with me, he called a friend of his in Bonnyville who then called me and told me I had no right to forbid him to come home. However, I told him I was not going to change my mind so his friend said he would give him some money to live on "because he's got to eat!" Oh my goodness, I hadn't even thought of that.

He got a motel room near the hospital and the plan was to see the doctor every day and get back on his meds. His friend gave him money to pay for the motel and to buy food. This arrangement lasted two days. He then called his parents in Indiana and told them he had no place to go. He asked them if he could come live with them and they agreed. His mother called me and told me that I obviously didn't know how to take care of him. She assured me she would return him to full health. Her remark filled me with anger and frustration but I felt it was best to just let it go. She would find out in time.

During this time period I contacted an attorney to file for bankruptcy. I also spent a day closing up the Bonnyville office with the help of his dental assistant. When he showed up at our house to gather his belongings, he begged me to let him stay and start over. However, I held firm and told him no, he had to leave. So he packed up his car with as much as he could put in it. I told him I'd send the rest to his parents' home in Indiana. Finally he got into his car and tearfully drove away yelling out the window to the kids, "Daddy will be back!!"

It was over. My nightmare had ended. Feeling like I was a prisoner in my own home was now behind me. Unlike the mind-numbing fear I felt when my first husband left me, this time I was relieved and totally exhausted. The days of debilitating back spasms caused by tension were behind me. The days of dreading Tuesdays when he returned home from his other office were a thing of the past. No longer did I have to cover for him and attempt to act as if everything were okay to my friends and neighbors. And no longer did I have to console the office staff when he didn't show up for work. I was 43 years old and it was time to rebuild my life and start over........again.

Chapter 5

Starting Over for the Second Time

I t was August of 1986. Although Stacey was married and had moved out of the house, I still had Andy and Ashley to provide for. The only income I had on my own was the small monthly check I got from the Village of Bonnyville for my part time job as a home-based police dispatcher. I had taken on that job a few months earlier but it would certainly not be enough to support me and the kids. Plus a few checks came in from patients who were paying their bill but that would end soon.

My counselor enlisted the help of Camille, a counselor from the Mental Health Department, to take me to the Department of Social Services to help me apply for financial assistance. My counselor told me that when the interviewers see Camille, her presence immediately alerts them to the fact she is escorting an emotionally fragile person and they treat her client with a bit more patience and kindness. I was confident I could handle the process on my own and didn't need Camille's "protection" but I went along with it to please my counselor. I had to sign papers indicating I would pay Social Services back when I sold my house. I answered question after question after question and carried with me a bulging envelope full of the required documents. After awhile Camille could see I was doing fine on my own so she told me to go see the last interviewer on my own. This one was about child support. When the interviewer asked me if I knew where Andy's father was so they could go after him for child support, I rolled my eyes and said I had no idea. This infuriated him and he leaped to his feet and leaned over the desk and yelled at me that this was serious and to stop making light of the situation. I immediately dissolved into tears and burst into uncontrollable sobs. He quickly sat down and told me to sign some papers. I couldn't read them through my tears but I signed everything anyway. I was excused from his office a short time later. I was still crying when I walked over to Camille who was sitting in the waiting room. When I told her what had happened, she became furious and said she wished she had gone in with me. She assured me his outburst would never have happened if she had been sitting beside me. As Camille drove me home a short time later, I fell apart again. This time it was because we were driving past several lovely houses. I looked out the window and sobbed, "I will never have my own house again. EVER!!" At that point it became clear to me why my personal counselor had asked

Camille to drive me that day. I wasn't as stable as I thought I was. I'd been strong and had been holding it together but I reached a breaking point that day. I couldn't stop sobbing. I couldn't catch my breath. It felt as if all the life slipped out of me in that ride home and I could not get myself under control. While I screamed and sobbed, Camille calmly and quietly kept driving me home. My heart was broken because I wanted to live in my house with my family and now it was gone forever. I couldn't bear the pain of such a significant loss.

I should have started beating the pavement looking for a job at that point but I was not yet capable of tackling a full time job. I was mentally exhausted and drained so I was grateful to receive an invitation from a woman in my church who ran the community preschool to work a few mornings a week helping with the children. At least that would provide a small income and give me a routine to follow by giving me a place to go four mornings a week.

I put the house on the market but was unable to sell it. Since I was not making mortgage payments, it eventually went into foreclosure, but the bank had allowed us to live in our home one final year. As that last year drew to a close, I began looking for an apartment for the three of us. The thought of moving was made easier by the fact that repairs and yard upkeep became an overwhelming job that year. I published an article in a magazine called *Christian Single* in 1993. It described the pain of sorting through the decade of "treasures" I had gathered as I prepared to move into much smaller living quarters. By the time I had sorted through all of the items we had stored in the basement, the garage, and various closets, I came to the conclusion that it was far better (and more permanent) to store up our treasures in heaven instead of the basement.

As my search for our next home began, I started each morning with my prayer wish list. Could I please have an apartment in a nice neighborhood with nice neighbors. I would like space for my washer and dryer so I wouldn't have to go to the laundromat. I would like three bedrooms. It must allow pets since I had a cat. I kept looking at apartments but couldn't find the right one. One day I mentioned to one of the mothers who came to pick up her son from preschool that I was looking for an apartment and she said her husband was renovating a duplex on East Main Street and that it would be ready for occupancy very soon. I took a look at it and there is was. There were three bedrooms and a bathroom upstairs. Downstairs a large carpeted room that had once been a kitchen and dining room had been transformed into one really large living room. The kitchen was quite large because it had once been the living room. Now it was equipped with new cupboards, a new stove, and a new refrigerator. A new cutting board countertop on either side of a stainless steel sink completed the renovation. In a corner of the large kitchen was a place for a washer and dryer. My side of the front porch had adequate space for a couple of chairs and a small table and it overlooked my section of our little front yard. Could I bring my cat? Yes, the landlord said. No dogs, but cats were definitely allowed. Except for a few houses, most of my neighbors had lovely big homes with beautiful yards. Perfect.

In August, exactly a year after my husband moved out of our house, the kids and I moved into our three-bedroom duplex apartment. That month Andy turned 16 and Ashley 11. Even though our new apartment was nice, Ashley and I missed our old house and neighborhood. Frequently, I would spot her lying on her bed looking out the window which faced the river. Home to her was on the other side of the river. She would lie on her stomach and just stare out the window as big tears rolled down her cheeks. It broke my heart but there was nothing I could do to make it better. I was having my own struggles.

While attempting to appreciate my new home, I found I missed the privacy of sitting in my pajamas on my back porch where I could have quiet prayer time or study my Bible as I sipped a cup of tea in the morning. I missed the convenience of driving into the garage when it was pouring or snowing and knowing I didn't have to face the elements once safely inside. Now I had to carry bags of groceries through the pouring rain or across an icy sidewalk until I reached the protection of the front porch I shared with my next door neighbor. I missed having a laundry room where I could shut the door and not have to hear the clothes thrashing around in the washer or dryer. Now my washer and dryer were right in the kitchen. Having only one bathroom was another adjustment. Most of all, I missed the privacy that comes from living on a quiet street. Now I lived on Main Street and people were always walking by or driving up and down the street. Sometimes in the wee hours, drunks would stagger by yelling profanities. There was no back yard in which to put a lounge chair and enjoy a sunny day in peace and quiet. If I wanted to take a bag of trash to the garbage can on the front porch while still in my bathrobe, I always peeked out the door and looked around first to make sure no one was walking on the sidewalk or driving by. Andy, on the other hand, loved it because he was so close to town and could hang out with his friends more conveniently. Plus he was now within walking distance of his job as a clerk in one of our grocery stores. He thought the new location was totally cool.

After moving our possessions to the apartment, I held a moving sale at our house and sold all of the items I no longer wanted or had room to take with me. For two days they swarmed through the rooms of my house and I watched my "treasures" go out the front door in the arms of their new owners. Finally, it was over. I slowly walked from empty room to empty room. Several emotions struggled within me. I felt grief for being forced to leave my home of many memories. I experienced the exhilaration of freedom when I remembered I would no longer have to struggle with snow removal or grass cutting or mortgage payments and taxes. I also felt gratitude for the Lord's loving provision of a new home for us.

As we were getting settled in our new apartment and figuring out where to put things, workmen were hanging from ladders outside our windows. It was not unusual to be startled by a stranger's face in a window as I walked around the apartment.

Plus our landlord came over daily to help me set things up and to check on my progress. Every day was filled with noisy chaos and a sea of new faces passing by my door on Main Street. All of a sudden I felt the overwhelming urge to run away and get away from people and confusion. Then I remembered a newspaper article I happened to see when I was packing up items in the house. I had grabbed some newspaper to wrap up a glass vase when I noticed a full page story about a place not far away called The Hermitage run by Franciscan monks. I quickly found the article that I had tucked away just in case and as I read the description, I knew I had to go there....soon!

The article described a peaceful retreat from the world in a wooded setting. Each guest had their own private tiny cabin. It had one room and a bathroom. There was a single bed, a tiny table for one, a wooden rocking chair, a small kitchen area, and a wood burning stove for heat in the winter months. There was also a tiny bathroom with a shower. Guests had to pump their own drinking and cooking water. The kitchen had a couple of plates, bowls, cups, and some silverware and a small supply of cooking pots and pans. The article went on to say that guests were instructed that talking to others was forbidden and that if they should pass each other on the path in the woods, a smile and a nod was all that was allowed or expected. There was a small rustic chapel for prayer if guests wanted to use it. The grounds were large and guests were encouraged to roam as far as they wanted. This was exactly what I needed. I called to find out what it cost (whatever I could donate) and when I could come (any time I wanted). I was just required to bring my own food, which I would cook on the stove in the little cabin.

The weekend of my retreat finally arrived and I couldn't wait. First I dropped Ashley off to spend the weekend with Stacey and her husband. Then I drove to The Hermitage. When I arrived, the first thing I saw was a long driveway with big iron gates at the entrance. I drove through the gates and parked the car. I got out and looked around at the beautiful wooded area that surrounded the office building and parking lot. As I stood there, a monk in a flowing brown robe came rushing out of the office and warmly greeted me with a big smile. He introduced himself as Father Anthony. Then he said, "Well, let me introduce you to...." and I inwardly groaned. Please no! I cannot meet or see one more person!! It turns out my cabin had a name and he wanted to introduce me to my weekend home. I was so relieved I almost started crying. He briefly explained where things were and then swiftly disappeared. I was finally alone.

I slept a lot that weekend. I took walks through the woods and smiled when I saw signs that said, "Silence is the language spoken here." I visited the little chapel whose pews were made of carved out logs. I wandered the vast area and would come upon statues in the middle of a well manicured field. I spent 30 hours in total solitude talking to no one but Jesus. I felt as if I began a new spiritual phase that weekend. It was difficult to return to the real world of noise and confusion and found myself whispering for the first few hours after I re-entered society.

As we adjusted to life in our new apartment, I tried to continue some of our traditions such as grilling hamburgers or roasting marshmallows on a little Hibachi on the front sidewalk, but it just wasn't the same as using a grill in our back yard. I missed all of my bird feeders but I no longer had any trees from which to hang them. At Christmas time, Andy and I discovered that the outdoor Christmas lights we had brought with us wouldn't work on our porch so outside decorating was now a thing of the past.

I soon discovered that life was still far from easy. Three months after moving, my station wagon ceased to be a functional mode of transportation. When my first grandchild was born that December, I had to borrow a car to drive to the hospital to see him for the first time. That began several years of driving $500 junky cars. One car was a Datsun that burned oil something awful. One night Ashley and I were in line at an impromptu parade to welcome our football team back from a victorious game and I had to keep turning the car off because the black smoke that surrounded us was beyond embarrassing. I owned another car whose frame snapped in half one day as Andy was driving it home after taking our trash to the transfer station. I had another car whose gas tank leaked so badly I couldn't drive it more than a few miles before it ran out of gas. I went for a period of time with no car at all (during one of the coldest winters in history, naturally!). I remember walking Ashley to the school one night to attend a Middle School dance and reminded her sternly to make sure she found someone to give her a ride home.

After a few weeks, a man in my church told our minister that he would like to anonymously buy me an $800 car that he knew was for sale. I was so excited! From that point on I slowly got nicer and newer cars but it took a long time and I spent many hours sitting by the side of the road waiting for help or having someone wire a falling muffler back into position so I could continue on my way.

Other harsh realities began to smack me in the face as well. Now that we had physically moved from our nice home to an apartment, my downsizing became public knowledge. It came as a shock to me when I realized my finances were so precarious I could no longer go shopping at the mall for clothes. I would have to rely on the church rummage sales and second hand clothing stores. In the past, our family had been one of the ones who donated food for the poor during the holidays and Toys for Tots at Christmas time. Now I was receiving food boxes.

When I filed my tax return, I was so excited to discover I was going to get a nice refund. I immediately started making plans on how I would spend it. But then I got a notice from the IRS saying they were going to keep it because of past due taxes. Our former accountant told me this would be the case for the next several years. I went home and bawled.

My New York State return was much smaller but I didn't get that back either. Since my unpaid NYS tax was less than what I owed the federal government, I asked my parents if I could borrow the $2,000 needed to pay that one off. They said no and suggested I ask our wealthy aunt, the one who had raised my mother during the latter half of her childhood. When I asked her, I was also turned down and told I should ask my parents for help instead of her. She said she didn't feel she could spare the $2,000 because she wanted to make sure she had enough money for her old age. (Note: When she died she left over a quarter of a million dollars to the university's athletic department and nothing to my mother or my brother and me, her only living relatives.) Finally, I got angry and took matters into my own hands and wrote to my state senator. I explained my desperate situation and pleaded for his help. I was totally shocked when I heard back from him and little checks of all of the withheld refunds began to trickle into my mailbox. Thank you Senator Cook!

Andy was beginning to be a bit of a handful. He dropped all of the good activities such as sports and band. Good friends were replaced with boys I was uncomfortable with. He started doing poorly in school. He wanted to get his license but I refused to let him get behind the wheel of a car until he displayed a more responsible and mature attitude. Naturally this infuriated him but I held my ground and eventually he earned my trust so I allowed him to get his permit and then his license when he was 17. I wanted to find a man in our church or community who would mentor him. He didn't have a father anymore and I wanted him to have a role model, someone who would take him fishing or something. Even though my husband had not been a very good or attentive father to Andy, there were a few times they did bonding activities such as playing golf in a father-son tournament. They did a father-son bowling tournament once too. Then there was the time he helped Andy with his Pinewood Derby car when he was in Cub Scouts. But now he had no one. At this time our church had a young minister who loved to work on cars. I asked him to help out and he agreed. I was delighted when, on a few occasions, he and Andy worked on cars together. But those times were few and far between so a strong bond was never established as I had hoped.

As for Ashley's recovery, I took her to an event called CHIPS – Christ's Helpers in Parental Strife. My mother had sent me a check for $100 to attend, saying she felt God wanted her to send this to me so we could participate. I remember it was a blistering hot Friday afternoon in August of 1988 when we boarded a bus for Elim Bible Institute in Lime, NY. We had to get off because it was too full. So we waited for another bus. The second bus had no air conditioning. We waited for yet another bus. Finally, a third bus pulled up and we left. We checked into our dorm room, which I remember had a floor that slanted and bunk beds. Ashley was so nervous about the weekend that she felt sick and wasn't able to eat the pizza they served everyone for dinner that evening. The next morning she still couldn't eat but I had no problem at all! They split us up into separate morning sessions. I was with other single moms and she was with other children whose homes had recently been upset by divorce or death. At last, Ashley learned she was not alone in what was happening in her life and tears of relief came spilling out. After the morning session, she felt a lot better and ate a good lunch at the picnic. That evening she made a friend and began to enjoy herself. The Sunday morning session was excellent and was followed by an amazing worship service that closed the event. I remember hugging Ashley tightly and crying as the song "Jesus Be The Daddy In Our House" was sung. The service ended with the children serving communion to their single parents. It was a turning point for Ashley and she began to truly heal from the loss of her beloved daddy.

A few weeks after moving into the apartment, I began my second year working at the preschool. The first year had gone quite smoothly. But several changes had occurred over that past year and my mind was clouded and crammed with worries about my future and my ability to support and raise my children alone.

Plus my closest friends, who had been such a huge support to me when I was going through the frightening dark days of Logan's illness, were now telling me they thought I should either take him back or leave Bonnyville. Go back with him? The thought almost made me physically ill. But I was a Christian woman. You don't divorce your husband just because he's sick, do you? What happened to "in sickness and in health"? But I had given it my all and it just wasn't enough. Had I failed somehow? I wrote a lengthy letter to a prominent Christian leader and described what life had been like and asked if I had to go back to him. I was desperate for someone to tell me it was okay to walk away from the marriage. I received a response that I should seek the advice of a counselor. After discussing my fears and doubts with my counselor, a wonderful Christian woman, she told me that I should never go back with him because it would be detrimental to my health and the overall well-being of our family. My friends had me so confused but I trusted her advice.

Apparently this preoccupation with doubts and fears was evident when I was at work because the preschool director came to my home on Valentine's Day evening and told me my mental stability was questionable so she didn't want me around the children anymore. I was out of a job! Once again I went into a deep depression and panic and had no idea what to do next. Ashley brought me out of it a few days later by asking me why I never laughed any more. Oh no! I couldn't do this to my child. How long had I been in this slump? I had no way of knowing but it was enough to kick me into a higher gear and I began to look for another job.

It wasn't easy since much of my personal life was far from a secret. I was the wife of the crazy dentist. No one knew that before moving to Bonnyville I had held a series of responsible positions at a major university and was actually quite capable. If I had moved back to my hometown, I could have easily gotten employment at the university again. But while moving back home was in *my* best interest, it was not in the best interest of my children and their needs came first. When I suggested one time that we might move back to my hometown, Andy told me he wouldn't go. To this day he doesn't recall ever making a statement like that but I will never forget it. Ashley simply cried and begged me not to take her away from her friends and all that was familiar. So we stayed in Bonnyville.

I applied at the bank, at the telephone company, at the school, and other places but no one was hiring. Finally, I was lucky enough to land a part time job working for our local weekly newspaper. I was still serving as a part time police dispatcher for the village as well. I was also continuing my weekly counseling as I attempted to rebuild my life and regain my sanity. I frequently attended 12-step meetings out at Tom and Rita's growing establishment and I devoured every piece of literature pertaining to recovery. I also joined a wonderful 12-step group called Women in Recovery as well as a Bible Study group. After working at the paper for several months, I began to write a weekly column about single parenting where I shared my experience and knowledge with the community based on what I had learned from the many books I had researched and my own life. I also started a support group for single parents that was fairly active for a year or so before it came to an end.

After a couple of years I discontinued my part time job as the police dispatcher and went full time with the newspaper. I was so glad to have the radio equipment removed from my apartment; at times it was a stressful job. In addition to answering calls regarding matters for the police, I also answered the ambulance and fire calls and sent our volunteer crews to medical emergencies or fires. On the lighter side, I was also able to use the position to my advantage on occasion. Once or twice when Andy had missed his curfew, I radioed the officers on duty to find him and tell him to get home. They cheerfully obliged!

My relationship with my in-laws had finally improved because they had to admit that even they couldn't make Logan all better. They discovered it wasn't my lack of care that had caused him to fail at leading a normal life. In fact, it was me who kept him functioning as well as he did for ten years before my strength gave out. They made a trip back to Bonnyville one weekend in the fall of 1988. They "exhumed" all of the bad memories I had buried. They asked me to drive them past the house, which was upsetting, but I did it to appease them. I answered their many questions and when they left at the end of the weekend they thanked me and said they now understood the entire situation better. Plus by then they had been living with their son for some time and could see how ill he truly was. For example, his mother told me that he had gotten a credit card in the mail from American Express. He began charging gas and several other items and ran up a huge bill. The problem was he didn't have a job and had no idea how the bill would be paid. Needless to say, his parents quickly took the card away from him. Making money and paying bills were concepts he never quite mastered.

I always thought it was interesting that although I was the financially stable one in our marriage, he was the one who was issued a credit card even though he was unemployed. On the other hand, I tried time after time to get a credit card but was unable to get approval because of my own income and past credit history. It wasn't until a credit card company finally issued me a pre-paid credit card that I was able to have my own credit card. I slowly built up my credit so that today my credit rating is at the top of the charts.

In the fall of 1990, Andy began attending a nearby two-year technical college and Ashley began high school. Ashley's high school years were busy with extra-curricular activities that kept me on the go. She was an honor student, was in the chorus, and played after-school sports.

Also in 1990 I got divorce papers in the mail from Indiana. Logan's family had decided it was time somebody did something and since I didn't have an extra dime to file for divorce, they took matters into their own hands and handled everything. I was very grateful to get that thick envelope stuffed with legal documents that indicated I was now divorced.

In May of 1992, Andy graduated from college with an Associate degree in automotive technology, moved back home, and found employment at a local dealership. Ashley began working summers at one of the nearby camps, a job that she loved and returned to every summer during the next few years. The extra income helped enormously because Andy began helping with the rent and Ashley could contribute to purchasing her school clothes. And then a welcome surprise at the beginning of Ashley's junior year in high school. Child Support! Throughout the previous years, I had received a bit of child support from my in-laws but now Logan was on Social Security Disability and Ashley was able to receive benefits until she turned 18. I received a substantial check in November for retroactive payments and I used it to buy us airplane tickets to go to Kentucky where

Stacey and her family were now living so we could spend Christmas together. This was the first time either Andy or Ashley had flown and I was thrilled to be able to give them their first experience.

And since this was Ashley's junior year, the big event was the Junior Prom. We shopped and shopped and shopped for the perfect dress but she couldn't find anything she liked. We then drove to Kentucky for Easter and, along with Stacey, we drove to Nashville where she found her dress! We were both looking forward to her big night on May 15 with eager anticipation. But then something happened I never imagined.

I was at work in the newspaper office on the morning of Friday, May 14, when I received a phone call from my mother that my father was dying in Florida. Stacey was already there, having decided a few days earlier to help my mother take care of him. *But the prom!!!* I had no choice but to fly to Florida that day with my brother. I hurried to the store to get red ribbon for Ashley's hair for the prom and then dashed home where I quickly packed a bag and drove to my hometown where my brother and I boarded a plane for Miami. I was so heartbroken to have to leave Ashley to get ready for her big night all by herself. She later told me it felt really strange to be getting ready for the prom all alone in the apartment. She went to the apartment house next door where one of the high school teachers was living and had her help her with her dress. I was torn to shreds inside at being away during such a crucial time in her life but I really felt (and still do, despite the pain it caused) that being with my mother, my brother, and Stacey at the time of my father's passing was where I needed to be instead of helping Ashley get dressed for the prom. I had helped her with all of the preparations leading up to it so she was good to go, but still......

There was no funeral. No memorial service. Nothing. A couple of tears were shed mostly for the sad life my father had led, not for any deep grief that he was gone. I was asked one time if I missed my father and my answer was, "No. I missed him my whole life." But shortly before he died, when I was 50 years old, my mother called me from their home in Florida and said "Your father wants to say something to you." She sounded .....what? Disgusted? Resigned? Anyway, due to his declining health he had difficulty speaking and he stuttered and stammered a lot, but he did manage to say he was sorry for the way he had treated me and that it was wrong of him and that he loved me. I don't recall my response. It was probably along the lines of "That's ok" but I doubt if I said I loved him. Maybe I did. I've forgotten.

Ashley's senior year was 1994 and it was an exciting time for both of us. She was looking into colleges but was struggling to nail down a major. She was a gifted singer and often sang the National Anthem at high school sporting events. She had a leading role in a school play where her singing was showcased. But when I asked her what she wanted to take in college, she'd just look vague and reply, "I don't know. I just want to be a famous country singer." Oh my. She applied at a few colleges and we went for auditions. She was accepted at more than one and decided on one of the prestigious colleges in my hometown because we were there so often that it was like a second home to her as well and she didn't feel comfortable going any place else. Since I had no money at all for college, she was eligible for all kinds of loans and grants and received scholarships as well. Years earlier Logan had told me that his older brother, who was quite wealthy, would be willing to help with college expenses if needed when the time came, but when I called and asked him for assistance, he got quite angry with me for even suggesting such a thing. Although I had enjoyed a good relationship with him and his wife when Logan and I were married, they now wanted nothing more to do with me or Ashley.

Her graduation was filled with excitement. We had a wonderful party planned for the day after graduation and she was going to be singing a solo during the graduation ceremony that she had been working on with her music teacher. She couldn't wait to have her father come and see her perform. She had stunned everyone in the last couple of years as her exceptional singing voice blossomed and became apparent. She couldn't wait to see her father's reaction. Although he had made a couple of brief visits a few years earlier, she hadn't seen him in a really long time and wanted desperately to share her high school graduation with him. The day before her Friday night graduation we got a call from his parents who told us that although they were planning to come, her father was not well enough to join them. Ashley was heartbroken and devastated. I felt completely helpless as I watched her double over and scream and cry after hearing the news that her father would miss one of the biggest nights of her life. I could only hold her sobbing body and reassure her I understood her pain.

By the next night, all of our family had gathered. Stacey was there from Kentucky, Andy was there armed with a video camera we had borrowed. My mother was there from Florida, and my in-laws were there from Indiana. I sat with my mother in the auditorium, Stacey and Andy stood at the back so Andy could tape the ceremony and Stacey could keep him company (and probably give him directions as well!). My in-laws decided to sit on the other side of the auditorium because the fans were blowing on them when they were sitting with my mother and me. Ashley's turn finally came to perform and she surprised everyone with her rendition of a popular country song called, "Letting Go." She got a standing ovation while I sat there and wept with pride. I learned later that my father in-law had nudged the person sitting next to him and proclaimed with a big grin, "That's my granddaughter!" She also walked away with the highest scholarship her high school offered. I was so proud I could hardly stand it.

So off she went to college in the fall but I didn't have an empty nest. Andy was still working locally at the car dealership and living at home while helping me with the rent. My assistance from the county had been cut drastically over the years even though I wasn't making very much money working at the newspaper. The county wasn't interested in that detail though. I needed his help to pay the rent. However, in April of 1995 Andy and several of his friends decided to go to Georgia and work for a road construction company to get the highways ready for the summer Olympics. They were an excited group of young men who were anxious to make the big money promised by the company. I figured I would manage somehow. The young men left in high spirits on April 22 but on May 3 there was a horrific accident when a speeding motorist went through their traffic pattern incorrectly and killed two workers, one of whom was part of the Bonnyville group, and injured two other Bonnyville boys. One of the injured was Andy. He wasn't hurt as significantly as the other young man but it still shook him up. The company paid to have Andy checked out and have x-rays just to make sure. The boys returned to Bonnyville for the funeral of their friend. Andy was then checked over by a doctor and declared physically fit, so a few days later Andy and his buddies returned to Georgia to finish the work they had begun. However, they were all emotionally shaken, especially Andy. The young man who had been killed in the horrific accident was Andy's roommate at the motel where they had been staying in Georgia.

But there was some happy news that summer. In August of 1995 my mother married John, a widower she had met about a year earlier. She was planning to have the big church wedding she never had. I was her matron of honor and John's son was his best man. There was a beautiful wedding cake, flowers, and a big reception with a live band. She wore a long sheath-style white dress with a wide-brimmed white hat. My daughters sang during the ceremony and at the reception. All of the children and grandchildren of the bride and groom attended the wedding except Andy, who was still working in Georgia and couldn't get away. My mother planned every detail right down to the place settings for all of the family members at the rehearsal dinner. She wanted us to all become one big happy family so she arranged for all of these grandchildren, most of whom were young adults with spouses and children of their own, to be seated next to a family member they didn't know. She wanted everyone to bond. This certainly did cause the grandchildren to bond. They were furious about being told where to sit. Who does she think she is? So in the end my mother won. They all bonded together as a group of grumbling young adults as they huddled together to complain among themselves about the injustice of being told where to sit. John and my mother had a delightfully happy marriage for 8 years before John died.

When I returned to Bonnyville after the wedding, life took a tragic turn again. Andy came home from Georgia and confessed to me he had been ignoring some pain for quite some time. He thought the pain he was experiencing was perhaps a result of the accident but upon further x-rays and tests, he was diagnosed with cancer. He had just turned 24. We were stunned. In early September he had surgery and I remember sitting alone in the waiting room while they operated. Finally he was transferred to the recovery room. The nurses led me into a large, cold, cavernous room of stainless steel where my precious son was lying on a table. He was barely covered with one thin blanket. He woke up soon after I entered the room and let me know he was cold. I immediately jumped into Mama Bear mode and demanded some blankets to cover his more than six foot frame. I remember him telling me not to touch him so I had to refrain from even holding his hand. That is pure agony for a mom who wants to hug her child. He was released the next day and came home to heal.

After his surgery, the remaining months of fall were spent making almost daily trips to a nearby hospital for chemo treatments. It was the most heart wrenching experience I've had as a mother and certainly one of the toughest things he had ever been through. He entered the hospital with a positive attitude that this was going to be something he could handle with ease. After the first few days of chemo, Andy began to get terribly sick and said he would not continue. He then refused to get into the car to go to the hospital. I called his doctor who spoke to him sternly a few days later and told him yes he would continue because he would be cured in the end. I wanted to take away his pain and felt helpless as I saw him losing his hair and growing thinner as the chemo took its toll on his body. By Thanksgiving the doctor declared him done with his chemo and on the road to recovery. Over the next several months Andy slowly regained his strength and we were encouraged by the good blood tests he was repeatedly receiving as well. We spent Christmas at my brother's house and by then Andy was looking much better. However, when we walked in my mother was nearly brought to tears because she said she barely recognized him.

After working for the newspaper for over eight years with no substantial raise in sight, I felt it was time to find a better paying job. Working at the paper had been perfect in many ways because the office was located within walking distance of my apartment as well as the high school. I never owned a reliable car so being able to walk to work was practically a necessity. Also Ashley could stop in on her way home from school when she wanted. Another plus was the fact that I occasionally took pictures for the paper. Since the paper focused on the events taking place in the school, I was able to go over to the school when they held a pep rally in the afternoon or take pictures on prom night. I took pictures of football games on Friday night and field hockey games in the afternoons. I didn't have to miss any of the extracurricular activities and got paid to attend them. But now Ashley was in college and I needed to move on.

I got a job working as the Purchase Manager of a manufacturing business located a few miles outside Bonnyville. The pay was a big improvement and so were the benefits. However, I was soon in over my head in the area of technology. We had not been given "real" computers when I worked at the paper. We had laptops and put our news stories on disks. The editor took these disks to the main office located 30 miles away once a week to download the information we had stored on the disks and then put the paper together. Now I was sitting in front of a big computer and I had no idea what to do. I was hired because of my shorthand skills and business training but I had no idea how to work a computer. Fortunately one of the other staff members took pity on me and explained how the various programs worked and I soon became reasonably proficient.

But it was one of the worst jobs I ever had. The factory was downstairs where the workers manufactured parts for rotary tools while the shipping department packaged them up and sent them on their way. Upstairs were the offices. We had an Export Office that handled overseas orders and clerical workers in another office who handled domestic orders that came in over the phone. My job was to purchase everything from pencils to large machinery. The owner came in once a week on a Monday. He was a millionaire attorney who lived in one of the New England states and had a summer home in the Hamptons. He would call about every hour throughout the day when he wasn't in the office and ask to speak to various staff members to either give them instructions or check on the progress of a project. It was a very interesting place to work in the beginning and I enjoyed learning about the rotary tool business.

But soon internal problems developed that made it a living hell. Bitter feuds erupted among the employees on an almost daily basis. Back-biting was a daily occurrence. In all my years of working in various offices, I had never experienced such unprofessional and childish behavior. After 4 ½ years, I had had enough and started to look for another job. But I felt those years had been valuable because they had honed my business skills that had gotten rusty during the decade I was a dentist's wife and they were hardly sharpened at all when I worked at the paper. Now I was computer literate and ready to take on anything. But where to look?

I started to look for jobs in a nearby city. I thought that I would move there since I no longer needed a three bedroom apartment. By now Andy had moved out and was on his own. Ashley had graduated from college and moved out west. I hadn't planned on staying in my apartment after my kids were gone. When I rented it in 1987, I told the landlord I just needed a place for a few years to finish raising my family. Well, I had done that. No reason to stay any longer. Plus Stacey was divorced and remarried and was now living in a nearby city and I wanted to be closer to her and my grandchildren. But I was unable to find anything in that city. Then one Sunday morning in church one of my friends said, "I heard Tom and Rita are hiring."

Tom and Rita? I know they had created a school in the last few years but I didn't think that sounded like a good prospect. I certainly enjoyed the 12-step meetings I used to attend out there but I wasn't sure it was a suitable place to work. I needed stability with a good income and benefits. I admired what Tom and Rita had established but was it for me?

Tom and Rita's commitment and dedication to help young people overcome their addictions became so well known over the years that more and more teenagers and young adults came to them for help. The demand forced them to move out of their home to a farm situated on several sprawling acres. After a few years the state insisted they educate the young people who lived there.

They sent school age kids into Bonnyville to attend the public school but allowing them to mingle with teenagers who were not in a 12-step program proved to be an ineffective way of helping them. In order to keep them on the property and give them an education, they needed to become an accredited boarding school. And they did.

Before it became a school, it was an oasis where I spent time in the late 80's and early 90's learning about myself and how to recover from my past. I remembered the entrance was a rather long deeply rutted dirt road with wide pasture land on both sides. There was a barn and a long white building where everyone met. Meals were served in a large dining room upstairs while downstairs there were small rooms for meetings and office spaces. A small room at the very top of the building served as the chapel. I had enjoyed going to the meetings or having dinner on occasion but I eventually began to focus on meetings in the village and discontinued driving out of town to the farm. The year was now 2001 and I hadn't ventured onto the property in over a decade.

But I finally decided I had nothing to lose by at least checking it out. When I turned off the highway onto the road leading to the school, the first thing I noticed was that the dirt road between the pastures of grazing cows was now paved. Acres of freshly mowed grass spread out on both sides. As I continued on, I noticed a new road to my right. I stopped and saw there was a beautiful chapel with a steeple nestled behind the trees at the end of the road. I continued along. I drove up a slight hill and when I came down the other side what I saw almost took my breath away. An impressive new school building was now sitting on top of a hill, its red metal roof shining in the sun. Beyond the school building was the original building I remembered from years earlier, but it had a new paint job and some major renovations had been done so that I hardly recognized it. On a steep back hill, there were rows of trailers that had been renovated to create dorms for the 250 or so students now in attendance. In addition, there were acres of rolling green lawn that included a soccer field and a softball field. Outside the school building was a basketball court. I parked in the large black-topped parking lot and got out of my car to look around. The well cared-for big red barn was still there and beyond that I could see a gorgeous pond. The entire property provided a breathtaking view of miles and miles of the rolling mountains. I couldn't believe what I was seeing.

I climbed the steep set of stairs to the school building. I opened the glass door and entered the foyer where a life-sized statue of Joseph holding the Baby Jesus was standing on a tall flagstone pedestal. I then opened the next set of glass doors and was immediately struck by the shine of the highly waxed floors. I walked past an extensive glass trophy case built into the wall and entered a busy office with six desks behind the two counters. This was not at all what I was expecting. After filling out the application and being interviewed a few days later, I was hired. I took a large pay cut but it was worth it to get out of my current situation and enter a spirit-filled place of employment. I began in May 2001 and have never regretted my decision.

Because it is a boarding school, staff is scheduled to work around the clock seven days a week. This was like no other office job I had ever had. I no longer had weekends off. I was expected to do office work as well as work with the troubled teenagers. Instead of working hard to make a wealthy man richer, I was working to save the lives of our endangered youth. At my previous job my co-workers found it amusing that I attended church every Sunday. At my new job, having a Bible in my desk drawer was practically expected. I could walk down the hall when the students were changing classes and frequently overhear someone say, "Have you prayed about that?" I had found my perfect job.

In addition, every day another lesson was learned as I listened to the staff counsel and instruct our students. It was as if I were attending a 12-step meeting all day long. I especially related to the girls who were boy crazy. Relationships were forbidden. The students were told they needed to learn how to just be friends with the opposite sex before going to the next level. Therefore, a family atmosphere was enforced and they were to think of each other as brothers and sisters. Over and over again the girls heard lectures about paying attention to their own needs and discovering who they were before venturing into a relationship. As I watched these girls struggle to become independent women, I wished I had had the same opportunity when I was a teenager. My teenage years were spent in constant turmoil as I searched for a boyfriend or held on way too tight when I found one. The times between boyfriends were frightening and lonely as

I desperately searched for someone to fill the void in my life. I wondered if the girls appreciated the wonderful opportunity and education they were receiving at the time. The boys were given the same lesson. I slowly gained confidence as the years went by and I learned more and more.

Chapter 6

Stuck in Bonnyville

Now that I had this new job, it looked as if I were destined to remain in Bonnyville. When I first moved to Bonnyville, I was determined to get out of there and return to my hometown as fast as I could. I hated Bonnyville. When Ashley was born and the school census was being taken, I answered the questions of the census taker as politely as I could but all the while I was thinking to myself, "There is no way this baby is going to attend kindergarten in Bonnyville!!"

To me, Bonnyville in contrast to my hometown with its several colleges and a major university was desolate and the environment itself was simply not stimulating. I was used to the world of academia and poetry readings and concerts. I missed what I felt were simply the basics of civilization such as several movie theaters, home-delivered pizza, take-out food and fast food as well as elegant restaurants. Plus I was used to huge fireworks displays at the university on the Fourth of July, large concerts, several spacious parks, and a large lake. I was accustomed to having the choice of shopping in several large clothing stores along with many well-stocked grocery stores and drug stores. I was used to a bustling city filled with college students. Bonnyville was one huge culture shock for me.

When I moved to Bonnyville in the mid 1970s, it had one movie theater, the diner was the only place where you could get a take-out meal, the fireworks display at the end of July in the little park was just a few minutes of small explosions, large concerts were held nearly an hour away in a nearby city, there was no restaurant that compared to the elegant restaurants we frequented in my hometown, and there was no lake – only a river. And parks? Bonnyville had one park which was nothing more than a small grassy area by the river. I was used to grand state parks with breathtaking waterfalls, gorges, and hiking trails as well as sandy beaches. It was several years after I moved to Bonnyville that McDonald's came to the village. There was one bank but a lot of bars and gas stations. There was one expensively-priced clothing store for women and a clothing store for men but no place to buy clothing for children. Bonnyville had one little drug store. To add to my misery, I missed my sorority sisters and our meetings and social events. I was surprised at how everything was on a much smaller scale in Bonnyville. Parades were a tiny little event, church services were small, and social gatherings were sparsely attended. I was not going to stay.

Now that my kids were grown and gone, I could go anywhere I wanted. I could return to my hometown! But to my surprise, I discovered Bonnyville was now my home. My hometown friends had led lives that were separate from mine for the last 25 years. I no longer really knew them and they no longer knew me. The only person I knew back home was my brother who lived in a small village situated a few miles outside the city. My friends, my history, my pain and my recovery were all centered in Bonnyville. Only my Bonnyville friends knew what I had gone through and had survived. And I had grown to love the mountains and the river that ran through town. I loved the people who had helped me through my darkest days. There was, of course, my counselor, who became a dear friend while helping me to survive. There was my neighbor who did charity work and brought me a pile of toys to give my grandsons when they were little when I couldn't afford any Christmas gifts for them. There was my church family who had given me hugs and prayed for me when things were tough. Another neighbor asked me what she could do to help when Andy was going through his cancer treatments and I told her I really wanted some homemade chocolate chip cookies. And so she went back home and baked a batch of my favorite comfort food. Her husband, who had a vegetable garden, still routinely leaves a plastic bag of tomatoes, cucumbers, and peppers hanging from the handle of my front door every summer. The dentist who took over our patients when I closed my husband's dental office told me my children and I could have free dental care for as long as we lived in the area. When I moved from my house into the apartment, several strong men from the fire department volunteered to move my heavy furniture for me and refused to accept anything more than a thank you. There were my Writers Group friends. And my Bible Study friends – both Catholic and Baptist. There were my prayer group friends. I didn't need to move and start over because these people were my friends and Bonnyville was now my home.

So I began my job at school and stayed in my 3-bedroom apartment. I filled it with cats and discovered it wasn't too big for me after all. I took over all of the closets and dressers and after awhile wondered how we had all fit in such a small apartment. I was no longer raising my children but I was still a single mom facing events in my children's lives all by myself.

Stacey:

When Stacey was 21, she set out to find her father. And she found him. He was living in my old hometown. He was married to his third wife by then. She was thrilled to meet him and found him to be delightful and full of fun. At the time she resented the fact I had kept her from her father while she was growing up. She couldn't understand not only the predicament I was in with Logan, but also the fact I had no idea for many years where Jeff was. A few years later when she and her husband were living in Kentucky, her marriage ended. She needed to return to New York so family members could help her get her life back together. Somehow she managed to get in touch with both her father and my mother (who still detested each other) but who pooled their money to buy her and her young sons airline tickets to return to NY.

One night after she had been settled in her new environment for several months, she got to thinking about her past and went to her father's apartment for a show-down. Stacey was mad that her husband had left her for another woman and now she wanted some answers from her father for his behavior. Jeff was no longer living with his third wife and was raising Jonathan, the son he had with Sandy, who was now a teenager. She pounded on his apartment door. When Jeff let her in she demanded to know why he had abandoned the family when she was little. Jonathan emerged from the bedroom and ordered Staccy to stop screaming at his father, to which she replied, **"YOUR** FATHER??? HE WAS MY FATHER LONG BEFORE HE WAS YOURS!!!" From what she later described to me, Jeff calmed them both down and sent his son back to bed while he agreed to sit down and answer all her questions and hear all of her complaints. I would love to have been a fly on the wall that night.

Andy:

In the fall of 2004 Andy was putting together a small cabinet for me when he complained of a pain that had been bothering him. I urged him to go see a doctor ASAP. When he got the results of his blood work, he discovered he had cancer.....again! This was not supposed to happen. This type of cancer was curable!!! The situation this time around was quite different from when he was 24, single, and back home with me. Now he was 33, owned his own home, had a job, and had a wonderful woman named Cindy in his life. Cindy would now bear the brunt of what was to come and she had no idea what lay ahead. Actually, none of us did, but she became the family cheerleader telling us it was going to be okay and that he was going to be fine and not to worry. But this time the treatment was ten times worse and if it hadn't been for Cindy urging him to keep going, he would have quit and we would have lost him. The chemo treatments this time were extremely intensive and required him to stay in the hospital for several days at a time. Once he had regained his strength from the chemo treatments, he went to Sloan Kettering Memorial Hospital in NYC where they removed all of the lymph nodes in his chest. He was out of work for a year. Family members sent him checks from time to time to help him pay his bills and stay afloat until he could return to work. He is now fully recovered but he said that if it comes back a third time, he's done. No more treatments. But he'll never have to face that decision because he has a mother of tremendous faith who prays every day that the cancer is now gone for good.

Ashley:

Ashley decided she wanted to live out west after she graduated from college. Following a year of planning and saving her money, she bought a reliable truck, adopted a Golden Retriever puppy, used the internet to secure a job and a place to live, and in May of 1999 off she went in search of new adventures and a cowboy. I was terrified but she was a 22-year-old college graduate so I no longer had much say in how she lived her life. She spent the next couple of years living out west traveling between Wyoming, Arizona, and Colorado. She tended bar at a steakhouse that was frequented by the rodeo riders. She made a lot of friends and met a lot of cowboys. One night she was even asked to sing the national anthem at the rodeo. Wearing a cowboy hat and cowboy boots, she and her trusty dog spent many days happily exploring the area while driving around in her truck. However, her dream of finding a cowboy didn't work out and she had her heart crushed and broken.

After leaving Wyoming and traveling to Arizona in the winter with her rodeo friends, she met a nice young man who was not a cowboy. In fact, he was a high school English teacher. Ashley introduced him to me when I flew out there to visit and I immediately knew he was going to be *the one.* In October of 2001 Ashley called me from Arizona to announce he had proposed. I was so delighted. She wanted to get married in my hometown and was hoping her father would be well enough to walk her down the aisle. He had missed her high school graduation as well as her college graduation but we hoped this pattern wouldn't continue for her big day in June. She picked out her wedding gown in Arizona and had it shipped to a bridal shop in upstate New York. Stacey and I drove there to pick it up and I found my own dress as well. I helped with Ashley's wedding preparations as much as possible but at the age of 25, she was quite capable of putting it together herself.

When the big day finally arrived, her father did indeed show up and walk her down the aisle although he came without his parents. Ashley's grandfather had recently died so her grandmother didn't feel ready to travel. Logan was extremely nervous and uncomfortable and refused to attend the rehearsal and rehearsal picnic at my brother's house the night before. I have a feeling he was uncomfortable to be in such close quarters with Stacey, Andy, me, and the other family members after so many years of separation. I didn't see him until the day of the wedding. We were in the basement of the church getting ready for the wedding. I came out of the ladies room and literally ran right into him. I had heard his medications caused extensive weight gain but it was still a shock when I saw him. I smiled and said a cheerful "Hi" and he responded "Hi" back to me and then we went our separate ways. That was the only time we spoke all day. He had a lady friend with him, who did her best to encourage him to smile after the ceremony when we were asked to pose for the wedding pictures. I felt bad for Andy when he told me afterwards that he had called out to his father during the reception by saying, "Dad! Dad!" and there was no response. Finally he called out "Logan!" and his dad looked in his direction. It was clear that Logan no longer knew the son who had become a man.

Chapter 7

Let Me Titus You

Years ago when I was a stay-at-home mom, I was a faithful listener to a popular Christian radio station. As I went about my daily routine, I would enjoy hearing Christian music as well as sermons and Bible studies. One morning while listening to a broadcast of Chapel of the Air, I heard Karen Mains say she wished she had someone to Titus her. She went on to explain that in Titus 2:3-5, Paul instructs Titus to encourage older women to train the younger women. Karen Mains said she yearned for an older woman to mentor her as she struggled to balance her busy life being a wife and a mother with her activities outside the home. Since I was in the same position at the time, I completely understood what she meant. Now that I am an older woman, I feel it's my duty, my responsibility, and my honor to Titus younger women.

Speaking from my own experience, I think Christian women can be too hard on themselves. After I married the second time, I felt the need to present a wonderful Christian family to the world. I was not attempting to achieve perfection, but I wanted to come as close as I could. I found out God has His ways of humbling us, sometimes with hilarious results.

One warm Sunday morning, I drove my three children to church. Everyone was dressed in their Sunday best and every hair was in place. I was proud. I was doing such an amazing job. I pulled up to the curb and parked in front of a house that was next door to our church. A woman I vaguely knew was sitting on her porch. I smiled and waved to her, hoping she was noticing what a nice family I had and what a great mother I obviously was. Plus, I was smug. WE were going to church but obviously she wasn't. Tsk Tsk. With head held high, I ushered my children up the sidewalk and into the church. When church was over, I chatted with my friends for a bit while my kids dashed back to the car. When I got to the car, my darling children were screaming at each other about who got to sit in the front seat. Within seconds I lost my temper and started screaming at them to stop screaming at each other. After I got them quieted down, I glanced out the window, and there she was: the woman who didn't go to church. She was sitting there watching us. She saw my flailing arms and heard me screeching. Sigh. My secret was out. We weren't perfect after all. (I found out years later that the woman was a Catholic so she had probably gone to church Saturday night.)

Being a Christian woman, I questioned if I were perhaps obligated to stay with my husband if he got back on a regimen of taking his medication. The mere idea of living in the same house with him again simply terrified me. Although there had been a couple of times he smacked or shoved me, I didn't think I was in danger of being physically abused. So what grounds did I have to keep the door locked? Was mental abuse a good enough reason? And maybe I had been asking for it. Maybe I deserved being mentally abused because I could no longer bring myself to act like a loving wife. What if I would be affectionate? Would he respond in kind and would it then be all better? But I couldn't stand him anymore. It didn't help that some of my closest friends insisted I was making a mistake and should either go back with Logan or move out of Bonnyville and start over somewhere else. What a terrible Christian I must be! WHOA!!!

Fortunately my counselor made me realize that my husband was now a very sick man who would never be well enough to return to work and live responsibly. I had, in effect, kept him going so he could enjoy a normal life for ten years. She pointed out that I had provided a stable environment which allowed him to function as a dentist, husband, and father. I could not be expected to do it any longer. It was now time to concentrate on repairing any damage caused to my children and guide them the rest of the way to adulthood. Any other choice would be detrimental to their well-being. That was all I needed to hear. Having happy and healthy children was my priority.

I have always depended on God to guide me through life, but I don't think I have ever clung to Him as hard as I did that last year I

lived in my house. *I was so scared!* In my hours of quiet desperation, I would shut my eyes and imagine myself as a small child sitting on Jesus' lap. I would feel the comfort of His strong arms around me. I buried my face in His shoulder and sobbed. *Please help me! I don't know how to do this!* I didn't want to leave my house. I didn't know where to go. I didn't know where to even start looking. How were we going to live? What would I do for money? I wanted someone to take this nightmare away and make it all better. Day after day I begged God for strength and guidance. The clock kept ticking as the time for us to leave drew closer and closer.

God knew I was not going to leave my home willingly, so He nudged me out much like a mother eagle encourages her young to leave their nest. A mother eagle doesn't kick her young ones out of their home. Instead, she makes the nest uncomfortable by gradually removing feathers and other soft material. In the end, they become almost eager to leave. Likewise, the Lord allowed my "nest" to become uncomfortable that final year we lived there. During that last winter in our house, we had so much snow that I had trouble getting out of my driveway. In March, the snow thawed and the ceiling in the den began leaking. In the spring our above-ground pool collapsed and all of the water spilled out. In the summer I struggled to get the lawn mowed, plus several minor repairs became necessary, and I couldn't do them myself or afford to have them done. Although I was still not eager to leave my home, I was at least no longer devastated by the thought.

At the end of May, Logan came for a visit and I was a nervous wreck. Ashley, who was 10 years old, was thrilled and gave him a big hug. Andy, 15, was reserved and shook his hand. We all went out to dinner. Afterwards the kids went off with their friends and Logan went to the bar. He came home after 11 p.m. and was obviously drunk. He slept in the spare bedroom and I slept in my room. The next day he told me that we should get back together and he should start up his dental practice again in Bonnyville. I told him it was impossible because his reputation was now completely ruined. Once again he went out drinking after dinner. When he came back he said his friends at the bar said I was all wrong. He pointed out how it was too bad his friends were supportive while his wife wasn't. Before going to bed that night, Ashley cried over the fact Logan was leaving the next day. At some point during the night, she came to my bedroom crying and crawled in bed with me. I tried to explain to her why we couldn't get back together as a family. She tried to understand and it broke my heart. But I was secure in the knowledge I was doing the right thing.

Another thing I did right was not moving from Bonnyville. I had learned that **single parents should make as few changes as possible in their children's lives.** I couldn't change the fact our income was now drastically reduced. I couldn't change the fact we had to move out of our house. I couldn't change the fact their friends knew our family was going through a crisis. But I could keep them in their comfort zone and that's what I did. Maybe they would have been fine if I had moved them back to my hometown but I didn't want to take the chance that they might not have been.

It's important your children know you are still their parent and in control. That is also something that didn't change. They had the security of knowing I was in charge and they were held accountable for their actions.

One night while we were still living in the house, Andy, who was by now a 6' tall teenager, had been told he couldn't go out. I sat in my chair doing needlework as he stormed through the house, slamming things around. Suddenly he bolted for the door and slammed it behind him. I thought to myself, "Well, that's just great, but I'm not going to go running after him." After several minutes he came back in and went upstairs to his room without another word. I eventually found out he had gone outside and walked around the yard for a bit before heading to the garage where he sat in my car for a few minutes. I chalked that experience up to the fact I must have built an invisible fence around our home over the years.

Andy turned 16 shortly after we moved into the apartment that summer and expected to get his learner's permit and start driving. I told him that he was not going to get a permit until he started acting more responsibly and doing well in school simultaneously because driving was a privilege not to be taken lightly. He was furious but I held my ground. He was going through phases of acting responsibly around the house (making his bed, observing his curfew) but then he was failing a couple of classes in school. Then it would go the other way and he would do well in his classes but miss his curfew or skip a day of school. I was getting confused trying to keep track of what he was doing right and doing wrong and when he was doing it. So I tried another technique -- the poker chip jar.

I put a jar on top of the microwave and told him that he needed 20 white poker chips before he could get his permit. Every time he did something good (make his bed, pass a big test, help around the house) I would toss in a white chip. If he did something mildly bad I would put in a 5-point red chip, which meant five white chips were now added to the total needed for a permit. If he committed a major offense, I would add a 10-point blue chip. That would mean an additional 10 white chips were now needed. When the jar had the correct number of white chips, he could get his permit. He let me know he thought it was a stupid idea and he wasn't going to pay any attention to my silly little jar. He didn't even give it a glance when he walked past it. However, he <u>was</u> paying attention because one day he committed a minor infraction and I tossed a red chip in the jar and he got quite upset with me! Plus there were a few occasions I'd see him counting the white chips when he didn't think I was watching. It took an entire year but he did finally earn the right to drive.

Don't be surprised when anniversaries or holidays make you dissolve into tears. Whether you left him or he left you doesn't matter. What you are grieving about is what could have/should have been. The dream. The promise. I've had women tell me they are so annoyed at themselves for crying on their anniversary even though they are so glad they are no longer married and were so much better off. Yes, you are better off being out of a toxic marriage, and remember, it wasn't supposed to be toxic. You were in love at one time and it's very okay to grieve the death of a marriage that you had hoped would live on forever.

Expect sudden moments of loneliness to hit you unexpectedly. Although I no longer wanted to be married to Logan, sometimes I missed having a mate. One time I went to a Steve Green concert with my counselor and her husband. I had such a great time. It was spiritually fulfilling and uplifting, but at the end of the evening Steve Green encouraged all the couples to stand together for Christ. Everyone in the audience stood up and couples put their arms around each other. I saw my counselor's husband reach for her hand and I started crying. All of a sudden I felt so single, so alone. I didn't want to be with Logan, but the sudden feeling of isolation hit like a lightning bolt.

Feeling guilty about your choices. There were many times I felt guilty for giving my children the broken lives they had. Why didn't I marry a man who would remain faithful and help me to raise Stacey with self-esteem as she became a woman? Why didn't I marry a man who would set a good example for Andy? Why didn't I marry a man who was reliable and could provide for his family? If I hadn't chosen these men, none of this would have happened to my children. On the other hand, if I hadn't married these men I wouldn't have these children! Then I have to stop myself and realize this kind of lamenting is getting me nowhere. I made the choices I did based on what I knew at the time and the circumstances in my life. Sure I know better now, but I didn't then. I need to cut myself a bit of slack. I did the best I could.

Yes, I made bad choices. But I have great kids because I didn't let them down. I was there for them every day. And I am still there for them. My children have depth of character as a result of their struggles. It would have been nice to provide a "perfect" home for them with a loving mommy and daddy but even those seemingly stable homes no doubt have turmoil inside closed doors that no one knows about. Don't we all unintentionally damage our children to some extent? But the bottom line is, if you can honestly say you did your best and gave it your all, then your kids will just have to pick up the pieces and move forward with their lives. They can repair what is damaged and move past what can't be repaired. Let's hope they do it better when their turn comes to be the parent!

Join a 12-step group if possible and read Robin Norwood's book *Women Who Love Too Much.* If you are divorced, probably your emotional needs were not being met. There are so many circumstances that surround a divorce. Infidelity. Alcoholism. Drug use. Physical abuse. Emotional abuse. Mental illness. Pornography. If your husband truly loved you, he would have been kind, stable, and interested in you. He would have brought out the best in you, and you would have brought out the best in him. I've never forgotten the words a young man wrote to me in an email when he was dating the woman he eventually married. He told me that women have no idea how special they are. He said that women should be held in the highest regard and treated with respect and gentleness. When I went to his wedding, I was impressed with his young male friends who seemed to share his philosophy. I watched during the reception as his friends stopped and talked to girls their own age as well as women in their 50s and 60s. Sometimes they just sat and had a pleasant conversation. At other times they took them out on the dance floor. I overheard one of the young men excusing himself from a conversation by saying he had to make sure all of the women were having a good time. Needless to say, this young man and his wife have a very happy marriage. Even though they are now busy with young children, they go out of their way to make each other happy.

I joined Al-Anon and a 12-step group called Women in Recovery. Some of these women were recovering alcoholics and some were recovering from broken relationships. It is so helpful to hear other women express the same fears as you. It is so helpful to find out why your relationships turn out to be painful experiences. It is so helpful to find out there is a reason for why you feel the way you do. And it is so exhilarating to gain enough self-confidence that you can fly solo if that's what God has in store for you. It may be just for a time. It may be forever. But whatever the final outcome you will be fine with either one.

Chapter 8

Splashing in the Puddles

During the difficult times when I was so scared I didn't know how I could ever keep going, I cried buckets of tears. I mean *buckets!* Those tears turned into puddles that I almost drowned in but after I stopped crying, I decided to begin splashing. What exactly is that? I would define it as those moments in time when you suddenly feel free and self-confident. You are overcome with a feeling of exhilaration. You become almost giddy with excitement at having claimed your identity. For instance, it can happen when you're getting ready to go out the door and you take one more look in the mirror and realize you are simply no longer young and beautiful and your reaction is – "So what? I am SO happy with who I am now!" It's that delightful freedom that comes when you no longer care about impressing others or what they think.

I felt my first exhilarating moment when I recognized I no longer needed to be in a romantic relationship to survive or feel whole. I wasn't just trying to convince myself either. I really and truly felt it and meant it. Never in a million years would I ever have expected to reach this plateau. It was like finally breaking free of an addiction! I had never felt complete unless I had a man in my life, starting way back when I was a young girl and desperately in need of a boyfriend. Be happy alone? This simply could not happen. In the 50s there was a popular song called "Hello Young Lovers." *Don't cry young lovers whatever you do, don't cry because I'm alone; all of my memories are happy tonight, I've had a love of my own.* I remember hearing those words and shuddering at the thought of someone actually being content to be alone. She's alone and happy with her memories? Impossible! How could anyone be happy without a real person in her life?

But splashing in this particular puddle almost didn't happen. I did not date anyone after my husband and I went our separate ways in 1987. Back then, I knew I didn't want to get involved with another man, but I felt sad that I had reached this plateau. I recall sitting in my living room and leaning back in my recliner where I could see the birds happily flying around in the sky. As I sat there mesmerized, I noted to myself that even birds flew in pairs. I felt as if I were just observing life and no longer participating in it. I had no idea how to change it and accepted this status as my fate. But things were about to change.

Relationships. In October 2001, I got a letter in the mail from an old boyfriend. We had dated for a fairly lengthy period of time in junior high, but I eventually broke up with him. Even though I ignored him, he continued to have an interest in me. My mother thought he was wonderful and always hoped we would get back together. He and my mother developed a close relationship, but I was not attracted to him at all. When I completed my business school studies my mother arranged for him to drive to NYC to bring me and all my possessions back home. When I got home, I thanked him for the ride and that was it. We went our separate ways. I started working and he went to Viet Nam. Eventually he married and had a family and of course, so did I.

After I read his letter in which he said he would like to get in touch with me, I became curious to learn what he had been doing so we began to exchange emails. I found him to be completely delightful and extremely witty and humorous and some of his emails had me laughing uncontrollably. I was trying to remember why I had broken up with him so many years earlier. After corresponding for a few weeks, we made plans to meet at my apartment. He lived almost 200 miles away, but he was self-employed and could take a day off when he wanted.

We were both terribly nervous but after he had been in my home for a few minutes, we both relaxed and enjoyed catching up. Over soup and sandwiches in my kitchen, he told me he had never stopped loving me. Although he was married, he said his wife was mentally unstable and unable to work so he felt obligated to stay in the marriage. However, he pointed out that he lived in separate quarters in their home which allowed him to have minimal contact with her. In addition, each of his two adult children had serious issues that required his help, support, and guidance.

Since I wasn't looking to get married again, it didn't bother me that he was married. I was not trying to steal him away from his wife. I wasn't even planning to go so far as to call him a boyfriend since he lived so far away and we would not be seeing each other very often. I was impressed with his dedication to his family and touched that he never stopped loving me. He was just a long distance friend who brought some warmth into my life. As the weeks went by, we continued to talk on the phone and sent hundreds of emails as well. I found him so much fun to communicate with. What a nice guy! It was a delightful diversion to know there was a man somewhere who loved me and thought I was wonderful. I felt vaguely connected again.

But it wasn't long before I began to see another side. The person who I originally thought was humble and at times self-deprecating was replaced with a pompous know-it-all. I began to see an attitude of disrespect toward authority figures as well. In addition, his adult children were constantly involved in some sort of crisis that required his attention. Pretty soon everything about him started to annoy me.

One time we were sitting on my couch talking when his son called him on his cell phone. When he answered the call, he turned to me and put his finger to his lips to remind me to stay quiet. Excuse me? I'm not in junior high. I have enough sense to remain quiet while you're talking to your son, who has no idea you are visiting an old girlfriend 200 hundred miles away. I was immediately uncomfortable with the thought that we were sneaking around and doing something he didn't want anyone to know about.

Another time that he was visiting, I took him to a quaint restaurant for dinner and introduced him to the owner, who was also a friend of mine. As we sat at the bar having some wine, he started talking to her and before long he was telling her what kind of beer she should be buying and where she could get it. He was so pompous and full of himself that I was completely embarrassed. Meanwhile, she was the perfect hostess and acted impressed and interested in his entire presentation.

One day I excitedly showed him a video of Ashley singing the National Anthem at a recent Diamondbacks game in Arizona. When she had finished, I waited for him to tell me how wonderful she had done but instead he told me that his daughter was also a gifted vocalist and when SHE sang the National Anthem, she ended it with more of a flourish than Ashley did!!

He frequently regaled me with stories of how funny and clever he was at the expense of others. He enjoyed sending me off-color jokes on the computer. He was not interested at all in anything I had to say about my job, which I was eager to share. I was becoming enmeshed with my job and loved the school's mission, which I thoroughly embraced. I wanted to tell him about my experiences with the kids and how some of them were changing and growing and becoming amazing young people. However, somehow the subject always came back around to him or the 50s or some dirty joke.

As my spiritual life expanded, I began to find him less and less amusing. I realized I wasn't laughing hysterically as I did in the beginning. All he did was talk about himself. He wasn't in love with 60-year-old Cathryn Scott. He was in love with 15-year-old Cathryn Miller. Finally, one day after we had been seeing each other for about 4 months, we were sitting on my couch talking. I felt my eyes glaze over as I stared at him and listened to him talk. It suddenly came to me that I was bored and wondered why I was wasting my precious day off sitting there with someone I no longer wanted to be with. That revelation was so exhilarating. Here I was finally participating in life instead of just observing and I was not enjoying it as much as I thought I would. After he went home that day, I sent him an email telling him I did not care to continue our relationship. That was the last time I was ever even tempted to have a special male friend. I had been given an opportunity have a man in my life who said he loved me but I decided I didn't need it, didn't want it, and could breathe much easier without it. I was not trying to convince myself I wanted to remain single. I really meant it.

Young and Beautiful. Then there's turning 50. We still feel young at 50 but AARP sends you a happy birthday greeting and invites you to join their group. No way! I wanted to stay feeling and looking young. I joined Curves and worked out with a vengeance. Before Curves came to town, I worked out in my living room using videos. I lost weight and looked good. Because I have always looked younger than my actual age, I now looked younger than my 50+ years. But then I started to gain weight. I worked out harder. I gained more weight. I tried to eat healthier. No matter how much jumping and bouncing I did, the pounds kept adding up. I got discouraged and quit exercising. Eventually my doctor discovered I had an underactive thyroid and prescribed thyroid medicine. By the time the thyroid medicine kicked in, I no longer cared. I started wearing flowing tunic tops and accepted my new look. I continue to watch what I eat and I will probably start taking walks for exercise when I semi-retire, but in the meantime I'm comfortable with who I am and what I look like. I'm heavier than I'd like to be but I'm no longer gaining. I am not a young girl; I am not a size 10. I am who I am, and it's okay.

Besides our weight, which we supposedly have some control over, the next surprise comes when things start to sag. Some of the body parts that sag we can hide, but others we can't. Like the neck. Like the jowls. When I was in my 20s and 30s no matter how the camera caught me, I photographed well. I took it for granted and never gave it another thought. Then in my 40s I had to concentrate a bit more on presenting a good angle if someone brought out a camera. However, I lost weight in my mid to late 40s and regained a youthful appearance for several years.

Imagine my surprise in my 50s when I woke up one morning, looked in the mirror, and discovered that a change had taken place while I slept. After that, it seemed as if there was a new surprise almost every morning. My neck was starting to sag and get strange creases. My cheek bones disappeared, and pockets of flesh began hanging off the side of my face. Gray hair started to appear at my roots. My hands were wrinkly instead of smooth. My legs developed cellulite. I needed a face lift. I needed Botox. I stood in front of the mirror and pulled back the skin on my neck. Yes, there it is. There's what I used to look like. Next I would press my hands on my cheeks and pull them up. Yes, I recognized that person too. Where did she go? This went on throughout my 50s. Then I started noticing other women my age, and they had the same sags and creases. But I liked these women so much that it didn't matter. I really didn't even notice after a while. I now can look at the young women on TV or in magazines without envy. Of course they look beautiful. They are much younger. But, if they're lucky, their day will come when they are my age, and if they're smart, they won't mess up their bodies with plastic surgery and Botox. The looks caused by aging have become a badge of honor to wear proudly. I am older. I deserve respect for having made it this far. I am fine with my looks and no longer feel the need to wear turtlenecks in the heat of the summer.

Money. Does anyone ever have enough? Shortly after I closed the Bonnyville practice, a fairly new dentist in town gave me a check for $1,000 for Logan's Bonnyville patients' charts. It was a windfall. If he had given me a million dollars I couldn't have been more thrilled. I had no income and no money to live on. It was a Godsend. But then I got a visitor. It was the woman who used to work for us years earlier but quit when she couldn't handle the stress of trying to pay the office overhead after Logan cleaned out the checkbook. She eventually went to work for this dentist. In addition, a few years after leaving our employ, she and her husband bought the building in which we had our dental office. Our friends were now our landlords. When she got wind of the check I was receiving, she promptly showed up at my house and told me that we owed them $800 for back rent and utilities. I remember sitting across from her at my dining room table feeling totally defeated and exhausted. I slumped down in my chair and sighed, "Go ahead. Take it. Everyone else has taken everything from me. I no longer care." And she did. Although I had nothing and she and her husband were very comfortable financially and had been good friends of ours at one time, she took $800 and left me with $200.

I remember that if I had a $5 bill in my possession I felt blessed. When my bills came in the mail, all I could do was make little payments every week but nothing was ever paid in full by the end of the month. Now I can pay each month's bills in full and before they are due. I can afford to make modest car payments and drive a decent car. I can buy clothes out of catalogs or stores instead of rummage sales. I can put money in a savings account for my golden years.

Do I have enough? No. Not at all. I can't retire so I'm accepting the joy of being healthy enough to go to work every day. If I lose my health, I will deal with that when it happens. In the meantime, I am feeling very rich because I have enough to live on and enough to buy gifts for my children and grandchildren from time to time.

Cars. I had my own VW in the 60s and eventually traded it in on a newer VW which took me to work and Stacey to daycare. At some point Jeff and I got rid of that and got a VW van with a peace sign painted over the emblem on the front. After that we bought a sedan that was more suitable for our family. Then I had no car because Jeff packed the car with his stuff and left me. Then my mother and Troy got me a nice used car. Years later Logan bought me a brand new 1977 station wagon. By 1987 it was in such bad shape I had to have it towed away. Then began the years of driving one cheap piece of junk after another.

I created a lot of puddles crying over repairs and watching mechanics shaking their heads when they looked under the hood. I spent a lot of time stranded by the side of the road waiting for a tow. Then there was the day Ashley and I were returning home after her college audition in Connecticut, and the muffler began to drag. I pulled into a gas station and asked if anyone had wire or a coat hanger who could hook it up for me so I could make it home. There was the winter when I had no car at all because the frame broke in half as Andy was it driving home after taking our trash to the transfer station. I asked my parents if they would help me out but they said they couldn't. I remember looking with envy at the cars other people drove and wondering what it would take to own something nice and if it would ever happen to me.

My minister came to see me shortly after my car broke in half and told me that someone in my church just bought me a used car. I was so grateful. That car lasted for quite a long time. When my mother re-married in the mid 90s, she decided I could have her car since she and her new husband didn't need two cars. The beautiful white Oldsmobile Cutlass Supreme with burgundy velour interior was shipped to Bonnyville from Florida and for the first time in many years I had a nice car to drive. Andy fell in love with it immediately and asked me when he could have it. Years later, and after much badgering on Andy's part, I told him to find me a car I could afford and I would give the Oldsmobile to him. He found me a used Chevy Lumina and I gave him the Olds. Unfortunately by then, it had over 100,000 miles on it and gave him nothing but trouble as he kept putting money into it to keep it going.

A few years later, although my car was working fine and was almost paid for, Andy and Cindy needed a reliable vehicle as he underwent cancer treatments for the second time. So I gave them the Lumina and, with Stacey along as my adviser, found a replacement. A few years later, still unsure of myself, Stacey accompanied me once again to shop for a better car. Then in March of 2012 I went car shopping *by myself* and signed the papers for a pre-owned 2008 Honda. I did it!

Owning a House. I have been a homeowner twice and twice I lost my house. The first one was a 3 bedroom ranch-style house that Jeff and I helped design. When I walked away from my husband, I also walked away from the house and left him in it. I don't recall the details but I assume the developers took it back because it was eventually occupied by other families. The last time I drove past the house,

I was saddened to see my grandfather's beautiful hedges were no longer pruned and had grown tall and scraggly. Then I lived in a 4-bedroom Cape Cod that I truly loved. After living in it for eleven years, the bank foreclosed and we were forced to move into an apartment. The pain that caused was debilitating. I couldn't stop crying for months.

When I drove past the house, I'd recall some of my happier memories. The people who bought it completely renovated the inside as well as the outside and it is barely recognizable today. And then they broke my heart when they cut down Andy's tree. When he was in third grade, he planted a little evergreen tree for Arbor Day. He watered and nurtured it and years later it towered above the house. I loved seeing it whenever I drove by, and now it was gone. When my grandsons were little and came to visit, I often yearned to be back in my house where there was room for them to play inside as well as a big yard outside. I missed having the space to entertain my family for holiday meals. But then the years went by and my kids grew up and left. My grandsons grew up and moved out into the world, no longer needing space to play at Grandma's. And somewhere along the way the apartment became my home and I discovered I no longer harbored a deep desire to own my own house. Maybe it's because the need to create a nest is behind me, but whatever the reason, I enjoy watching HGTV without envy and I can in all honesty say I do not want to own a house ever again.

These are the things that made me cry, weep, and sob uncontrollably. The tears that created so many puddles are now behind me and I am stronger for having made it through the storms in my life. I consider each day, each birthday, as a gift from God. I am thankful every morning that I am able to get out of bed. I realize that more storms no doubt await me, but I'll get through those as well. I've already proven it can be done, but I have to admit I hope to continue splashing with reckless abandon in life's puddles just a bit longer.

Acknowledgements

Although I felt passionate for months about this book and getting out my message to other women, one day when it was nearly completed I almost decided to forget the whole thing. But then something changed my mind. A close friend died after losing her battle with cancer. Before she died she was a bundle of energy and power – all 5' and 100 lbs. of her. A little human dynamo and a force to reckon with for sure. She always used to encourage me to keep writing. During the eulogy at her funeral the priest said we should really go for it and *do what we were meant to do* just as she had always done in her life. Once again I felt my dear friend was nudging me to keep going so I put my doubts aside and moved forward.

But I didn't do it alone. I had the best cheerleading section and editors any author could ever ask for. Thank you Charlene and Aleta for your excellent red-pencil editing. Both of you threw more commas at me than I felt were necessary but overall I believe I accepted most of your editorial suggestions. Even though my two editors do not know each other and never met, they often made identical editorial suggestions. I figured if both of them said it then it must be right. Thank you both for your constant encouragement to keep going with this project and get it published.

Thank you to my mother who taught me from a young age to trust Christ and also instilled in me a positive attitude and instructed me over and over to stay strong and persevere during the hard times. Some days I got really tired of being strong but it did pay off in the end.

Thank you to my trusted counselor, Jan, who held my hand during the dark days of despair when I didn't know which end was up. Her quiet calm support through those difficult years was priceless. However, I was at times afraid that if she told me one more time to "hang in there" I was going to bop her one.

Thank you to my three wonderful children who have blessed me by becoming amazing adults. My oldest daughter has followed in my footsteps just a bit too closely but is beginning to splash in her own life's puddles. She is raising her youngest child as a single mom and doing a superb job. My son, who may physically resemble his biological father's side of the family, is fortunately nothing like him. He is a steady hard worker who has remained faithful to one woman for over 15 years. Turns out he didn't need a father to teach him how to be an honorable man. He just is. And my youngest child has made me proud by overcoming her childhood insecurities and shyness and becoming a confident woman who married her perfect soul mate. For the last ten years they have worked closely together to raise their children and build a solid life together. She is an amazing mother and wife.

And finally, thank you to my Lord and Savior who got me through the tough times and is with me now during these happy times. He led me to Westbow and for that I will be forever grateful.